ADVANCE PRAISE FOR *GROWING INTO EQUITY: PROFESSIONAL LEARNING AND PERSONALIZATION IN HIGH-ACHIEVING SCHOOLS*

By Sonia Caus Gleason and Nancy Gerzon

In Growing Into Equity: Professional Learning and Personalization in High-Achieving Schools, *Gleason and Gerzon provide rich examples of school-based practices that optimize professional learning and provide students with personalized learning opportunities. The detailed, insightful case studies illustrate what a visible commitment to equity looks like in high-performing schools.*

Bob Wise, President
Alliance for Excellent Education
Former Governor, West Virginia

Gleason and Gerzon focus their lens on four "regular" schools that are paying attention to the whole child and getting results. In these school communities, professional learning for educators produces personalized learning for students. Growing Into Equity *offers readers wonderful insights into the structures and strategies, time and talents it takes to make that happen.*

Randi Weingarten, President
American Federation of Teachers

Equity is not an afterthought to high achievement. Gleason and Gerzon's new book on outstanding equity-driven practice in four very different schools shows that if you want to raise the bar, you have to start by narrowing the gap. From Tennessee to Vermont, from Dallas to LA, this attractively written, morally uplifting and deeply practical book shows how extraordinary schools address and achieve social justice by making learning personal and engaging for every student, and by ensuring that professional learning is stimulating and practical for every teacher.

Andy Hargreaves, Thomas More Brennan Chair in Education
Boston College

Who says that schools can't personalize learning, improve achievement and provide an equitable and high-quality education for all students? As monumental as these goals may seem, they are possible. By highlighting four schools that do these things well, Sonia Caus Gleason and Nancy Gerzon provide a valuable lesson about personalized and equitable schooling and, in the process, remind us what public education should be about.

Sonia Nieto, Professor Emerita, Language, Literacy, and Culture
University of Massachusetts, Amherst, School of Education

Growing Into Equity *is a timely and important new book which provides compelling evidence of how teachers, principals, school district leaders and policy makers can create and embrace equity in school districts, schools and classrooms to ensure that all students are learning and achieving.*

Thomas Payzant, Retired Superintendent
Boston Public Schools
Retired Professor of Practice
Harvard Graduate School of Education

Excellence and equity in public school classrooms don't happen by accident. In this book Sonia Caus Gleason and Nancy Gerzon use detailed examples to show how sensitive, thoughtful and courageous leaders build school communities that favor every learner, including not only every child, but also every adult.

Ronald F. Ferguson, Faculty Director
Achievement Gap Initiative at Harvard University
Founder, The Tripod Project for School Improvement

Growing Into Equity *is both instructive and inspiring. Gleason and Gerzon emphasize the importance of professional learning, collaboration, shared leadership and a strong sense of collective accountability that envisions every student achieving his/her potential through personalized instruction. Should be required reading for anyone interested in transforming schools.*

Dennis Van Roekel, President
National Education Association

Growing Into Equity *dispels the notion of the principal or teacher as hero. It takes a team of people to raise achievement. It takes clarity of mission and vision. We are never "there" but always getting better—asking better questions so we CAN get better.*

Linda Nathan, Executive Director
Center for Arts in Education
Founding Headmaster, Boston Arts Academy

The authors delve into four schools—located in California, Tennessee, Texas and Vermont—revealing how personalized learning promotes equity. Their discoveries provide an encouraging roadmap for K–12 educators in urban, suburban or rural settings who wish to promote "favoritism" for each student. The core belief that "every child is a complex and compelling story as a person and as a learner" drives the need to personalize learning, and the how-to is well documented in this breakthrough work that provides hope the American dream may still be realized through public education.

Kathleen Sciarappa, Ed.D., Educational Consultant
Mentor Trainer and Coach for Principals and Aspiring Leaders
National Association of Elementary School Principals
New Hampshire Association of School Principals
Principal for 26 years

Growing Into Equity provides an essential understanding of how critically important it is for schools to both create and sustain conscious willfulness and intentional practices among all stakeholders. Growing Into Equity reminds us of the complexity of creating equitable learning opportunities in schools and at the same time provides diverse illustrations of personalized learning to move educators and students to that point.

Deborah Childs-Bowen, Ed.D, Chief Learning Officer
Alliance for Leadership in Education

The authors capture stories of caring, committed practitioners who challenge their students' thinking and excite their imagination.

Margot Stern Strom, Klarman Family Executive Director
Facing History and Ourselves

Many schools across this country are "doing" PLCs or data walls or walkthroughs, but adult learning activities have not translated into significant improvements in student learning. Growing Into Equity provides real examples from real schools where equity, personalization and leadership are enacted in every classroom in a variety of ways every day.

Jeanne M. Harmon, Executive Director
The Center for Strengthening the Teaching Profession

In a series of compelling and vivid case studies, authors Sonia Caus Gleason and Nancy Gerzon uncover a vision for education in which all students matter and each student succeeds. For anyone concerned with social justice in our nation's schools, this is a must-read book.

Margaret Heritage, Assistant Director
University of California, Los Angeles
National Center for Research on Evaluation, Standards,
and Student Testing

The book is an amazing compilation of real stories of high level practice in schools focused on the belief that all students can achieve and the extraordinary work of educators to ensure that the school accomplishes that task. This is a book written for the heart and mind of every educator. It is long, long, long overdue. It is not preachy—it is action oriented! I truly hope those that lead innovation and reform at the federal, state and local level will read this book to consider how real transformation takes place. Perhaps this should become a mandatory read for those dealing with reform.

Victoria Duff, Senior Consultant
Learning Forward
Former Coordinator, Teacher Quality
New Jersey Department of Education

This book provides concrete evidence through in-depth case studies of successful schools from different walks of life that the needs of all learners, students and educators alike can be met with an unwavering focus on equity and professional learning.

Melissa Kagle, Ph.D.
Assistant Professor of Educational Studies
Colgate University

"Every child is a complex and compelling story, and part of educators' work is to uncover their gifts," the authors write. With robust case studies, thoughtful analysis, and practical tools, the authors inspire and equip us to bring that statement to life. By examining professional learning that is tightly linked to equity and personalization, the authors offer their unique perspective on how to uncover teachers' gifts to serve each of their students.

Nancy Love, Director of Program Development
Research for Better Teaching

We find in these pages sensitive approaches for creating a culture of "high achievement, appreciation of individuality, and encouragement of lifelong learning" for both teachers and students. The inspiring examples of these four schools demonstrate what is possible when teachers and administrators collaborate in order to personalize instruction for every child.

Diana Lam, Head of School
Conservatory Lab Charter School

Growing Into Equity provides four vivid pictures of schools that have successfully responded to the elusive excellence with equity challenge that faces our public schools and society today. The four school descriptions that lie at the heart of this book bring to life those common elements—democratic leadership, focused professional learning, continuous improvement for individuals and schools and a thoughtful and intentional approach to whole school quality—that are critical for successful personalized learning for all students and teachers. The pictures of the four exemplar schools and the synthesis of the critical work by the authors have the power to provide both inspiration and concrete guidance in supporting our work to achieve equity and excellence for our students and teachers very, very soon.

John J. Freeman, Ph.D., Superintendent of Schools
Pittsfield, New Hampshire School District
Nellie Mae Education Foundation
District Level Systems Change Grant Recipient

The authors offer a rare view into the practices of the principal and teachers at Social Justice Humanitas that serves as an example to districts and schools seeking to increase school accountability as an outcome of districtwide reform: A continuous cycle of instructional improvement and personal reflection undergirds deep levels of personalization for students and staff alike. The process is intentional, methodical and uncompromising. As principal Navarro notes, "There are no short cuts to equity."

Jane Patterson, Ed.D., Senior Director
Transform Schools, Los Angeles Educational Partnership

For years, we've celebrated the power of focused collaboration. The authors share wonderful examples of effective practice that are accessible, inspirational and most important, actionable in our own schools . . . Each of the chapters is great! Really well presented.

Dr. Peter Dillon, Superintendent of Schools
Berkshire Hills Regional School District

This book shows a global need for rethinking the professional growth needs for educators and the leadership in schools to breed success for our students in the 21st century.

Karen Brainard, National Board Certified Teacher
Hilliard City School District

To my mother, Albina Vidas Caus, who personalized my learning with all that she was, while scouting out others to do what she could not, and to my father, Germano Caus, who taught me about exactitude and equity.

SCG

To my husband, Len, with enduring gratitude for the countless ways in which you recognize, honor, and cultivate the unique gifts and talents of the people you love. Through your nurturing of my strengths, over time, you've created the conditions through which this project could take root and grow.

NG

Growing Into Equity

Professional Learning and Personalization in High-Achieving Schools

Sonia Caus Gleason

Nancy Gerzon

Foreword by Stephanie Hirsh
and Joellen Killion

A Joint Publication

CORWIN
A SAGE Company

FOR INFORMATION:

Corwin
A SAGE Company
2455 Teller Road
Thousand Oaks, California 91320
(800) 233-9936
www.corwin.com

SAGE Publications Ltd.
1 Oliver's Yard
55 City Road
London EC1Y 1SP
United Kingdom

SAGE Publications India Pvt. Ltd.
B 1/I 1 Mohan Cooperative Industrial Area
Mathura Road, New Delhi 110 044
India

SAGE Publications Asia-Pacific Pte. Ltd.
3 Church Street
#10-04 Samsung Hub
Singapore 049483

Acquisitions Editor: Arnis Burvikovs
Associate Editor: Desirée Bartlett
Editorial Assistants: Mayan White and
Ariel Price
Permissions Editor: Jennifer Barron
Project Editor: Veronica Stapleton
Copy Editor: Terri Lee Paulsen
Typesetter: C&M Digitals (P) Ltd.
Proofreader: Gretchen Treadwell
Indexer: Gloria Tierney
Cover Designer: Edgar Abarca

Printed in the United States of America.

Library of Congress Cataloging-in-Publication Data

Gleason, Sonia.

Growing into equity : professional learning and personalization in high-achieving schools / Sonia Caus Gleason, Nancy Gerzon.

pages cm

A joint publication with Learning Forward and WestEd.

Includes bibliographical references and index.

ISBN 978-1-4522-8765-2 (pbk.)

1. Teachers—Training of—United States—Case studies.
2. Individualized instruction—United States—Case studies.
3. Public schools—United States—Case studies.
I. Gerzon, Nancy. II. Title.

LB1715.C37 2013
370.71′1—dc23   2013005353

This book is printed on acid-free paper.

Certified Chain of Custody
SUSTAINABLE FORESTRY INITIATIVE
Promoting Sustainable Forestry
www.sfiprogram.org
SFI-01268
SFI label applies to text stock

13 14 15 16 17 10 9 8 7 6 5 4 3 2 1

Contents

Additional materials and resources related to *Growing Into Equity: Professional Learning and Personalization in High-Achieving Schools* can be found at www.corwin.com/growing intoequity.

Foreword

Schools in which social justice permeates both student and educator learning are schools where students are not only academically successful, but also are transformed into leaders who aspire to practice social justice in their daily lives. Schools such as these emerge from the passion, purpose, and professional learning of their staff members. Authors Sonia Caus Gleason and Nancy Gerzon share stories of four schools in which staff achieve equity and model social justice through personalizing student and educator learning. The lessons learned from these schools provide concrete actions other schools can and should study for guidance in their efforts to prepare every preK through grade 12 student for college and careers.

Stults Road Elementary School, Social Justice Humanitas Academy, Montgomery Center School, and Tusculum View Elementary School have succeed by providing environments firmly grounded in shared values of equity and social justice and in the practice of continuous professional learning. Firm commitment to ensuring that every student achieves success provides educators with the impetus to break out of routines and commit to expand their knowledge, skills, and practices. This commitment also brings educators to question and clarify their personal and professional values and assumptions, challenge those that are barriers to student success, cement common values and goals among members of the school community, and unleash all possibilities to achieve student success.

In the communities where these four schools exist, student academic success moved from improbable to reality. These achievements are a result of educators learning and working together within a culture that valued continuous professional learning as well as enacting research-based practices of effective professional learning. Other schools can achieve similar results when they study and apply the standards for professional learning (Learning Forward, 2011). These standards define the conditions and actions essential to improving educator effectiveness and results for all students.

Professional learning in these schools provides exemplars of how the standards for professional learning are enacted each day. Educators learned in communities that use a cycle of continuous learning that integrates use of student data, frequent professional learning aligned with goals, and continuous assessment of the success of learning (**Learning Community standard**). Each school has strong leaders, both administrators and teacher leaders, who commit not only to build the capacity of all staff to learn and lead, but who establish the structure for ongoing learning (**Leadership standard**). While these schools are not unusually wealthy in terms of funding, they are rich in terms of resources of dedicated staff, often with coaches or other teacher leadership, time for teacher collaboration, technology, and other professional resources to support effective learning and instruction (**Resource standard**). The school models use student, educator, and system data to identify the focus for individual, team, and schoolwide professional learning to evaluate the effectiveness of professional learning (**Data standard**). In each school educators experience multiple forms of professional learning that address their individual, team, and schoolwide learning needs as defined by student achievement (**Learning Design standard**). Educators apply research about change as they sustain support over multiple years and ensure that educators receive peer and supervisor feedback as a lever for refining the application of professional learning (**Implementation standard**). Finally, professional learning in these four schools aligns to the performance expectations for each educator and to the curriculum students are expected to achieve (**Outcomes standard**).

Every student deserves effective teaching every day. Gleason and Gerzon show us that this is not a pipe dream. They provide four models of data-driven, personalized instruction that not only embrace the idea of equity, but also achieve it with all students, not just some, achieving high levels of academic success. By sharing and analyzing the professional learning practices at Stults Road Elementary School, Social Justice Humanitas Academy, Montgomery Center School, and Tusculum View Elementary School, Gleason and Gerzon provide readers with not only the inspiration to achieve this outcome, but also the guidance to achieve it by highlighting the unique and common attributes of professional learning that contributed to both student and educator success.

Stephanie Hirsh
Joellen Killion

Preface

It was not easy to find high-achieving schools with significant free-lunch eligible populations that also personalize learning across the board. When we asked educational leaders around the country to recommend schools, there were three typical responses:

> I know a teacher who personalizes for every student. She's/He's incredible;

> I know a private school that does that;

> I don't know any, but let me know when you find them.

Those answers reveal the reason for this quest. There *had to be* public schools where personalizing efforts led to outperforming other schools. And we wanted to know how they balance challenge and supports for students, and just as important, see how educators were challenged and supported to sustain and deepen that work over time.

The sparkly Sophia Nolan, who attends King Middle School in Portland, Maine, understood what this book was about right away. We explained we were looking for schools where every single student mattered and did well, whatever their background. She thought for a minute and then wistfully said, "Oh, you mean schools where there's favoritism for *every* kid." That's it, Sophia.

Every student deserves to be a favorite. And nothing less than an all-out effort to build professional capacity makes that happen. This book explores how educators at four schools learn, facilitate learning, and systemically grow into equity while personalizing instruction. It explores the professional learning, leadership, and systems that enable this to happen.

WHO WILL FIND THE BOOK USEFUL?

This book seeks to serve preK–12 educators and those who work with them. It particularly speaks to those interested in how equity leads to personalizing student learning in order to support maximize student potential, and can transform professional learning and leadership as part of that process. This book is written for the following:

- *School-based educators—teachers, teacher leaders, and administrators.* This book provides specific professional learning and leadership strategies with examples, strategies, and tools to deepen and extend capacity to help every student get what they need.
- *Professional development providers.* Professional learning practices, protocols, and routines encourage continuous improvement and reflection. They appear across the book and can be used both to help create a vision and to align and deepen current practices.
- *Teacher and administrator educators.* Professional learning and leadership are increasingly present in educator preparation courses. The cases here describe effective practices for individualized instruction and professional learning communities.
- *School board members and other policy makers.* This book's findings point to leadership and systems that enable personalization to happen systemically, so that successes are long lived and not reliant on individual school leaders' tenures. It can inform policies and practices for scaling up the work of equity and personalization.
- *District and state-level educators creating supports for school improvement.* These examples of school-based practices, along with the chapters on findings, provide specific scaffolds for district and state initiatives to provide resources and encourage focus. There are also accounts of particular ways districts provide both supports and freedoms that enable schools to be student centered.
- *Equity and change agents in school reform.* This book offers a vision and practical strategies for professional learning and leadership to advance equity through personalizing student learning. It shows how professional learning and personalization are effective, but emphasizes the specific ways an equity commitment can maximize the impact of these strategies.

FOCUS OF THE BOOK

This book sets out to answer two questions:

- What does professional learning look like in underserved school communities that are working systematically and successfully to meet the needs of each learner?
- What leadership and systems enable professional learning that advances equity and personalization?

We studied each school as a unit to understand how learning specifically works for both students and educators. We wanted to understand what conditions and practices made personalization work. The school cases allowed for a closer analysis of professional learning and leadership strategies that could be obscured in a broader district examination. They reveal specific implementation and professional learning issues that are more visible and immediately evident at the school level. Examination of these schools at work reveals what is possible, and it provides rich information for districts and states to consider when providing resources and guidelines to shape professional learning practice. Their work suggests avenues of research and advocacy for national reform.

DESIGN OF THE STUDY

This study offers four concise cases and complementary analyses that are the fruits of site visits using semistructured protocols and observations, documents review, and a cross-case analysis. Findings are related to professional learning practice. This research employed the case study method and cross-case analysis as laid out in the work of Miles and Huberman (1994). We relied extensively on interviews and observations in the four site visits, and extended written and phone conversations both before and afterwards. Site visits produced a wealth of student and professional learning experiences in action. In all, 23 educators were interviewed. This total includes interviews of seven school-based teams, as well as individual interviews and those with other combinations of educators. Nine teams were observed in action. There was also at least one classroom observation and a walk-through took place in each school, to counterbalance a focus on professional learning experience with exposure to student learning experiences.

From the beginning our intention for these cases was to capture, to the greatest extent possible, the perspectives and vignettes of educators, and sometimes students, revealing how learning and professional learning happens. An analysis follows each case, and examines values and practices in play, and systems that support those practices. We reviewed field notes and recordings independently and together, while one person took the lead on drafting cases and an iterative fact-checking and consensus-building process. One or more leaders at each school conducted a member-check, giving substantive feedback on both the case and its analysis, and sometimes offered additional artifacts or information to illustrate a finding. All those interviewed at the schools reviewed quotes where they were specifically named. We extensively used memoing in clarifying logistical process, summarizing findings, identifying gaps in information evidence, and considering angles of analysis in developing both the cases and their analyses.

The cross-case analyses were first based on a conceptual framework that appeared in a *JSD* article, "Digging Deeper: Professional Learning Can go Beyond the Basics to Reach Underserved Students" (Gleason, 2010). This framework spoke to the research-based fundamentals of professional learning: relevant and rigorous content, appropriate process, time, and supportive systems. It asserted that schools making progress with achievement while personalizing would also have deep attention to equity, use a range of data including formative assessment, and measure impact regularly and keep at it. The early findings of the cross-case analysis did not dispute the presence of these factors, but revealed an unexpected depth of and approach to these practices, and required reframing so this could come to light. Memoing continued to be important in this phase and was complemented by developing matrices that juxtaposed findings across cases. Quotes and vignettes were drawn from cases and school-based data that may not have made it into the cases, to illustrate points and offer a range of possible practices to make findings more accessible.

ORGANIZATION OF THE BOOK

The book features four high-performing, Title I schools and the practices and systems needed to personalize student and ongoing professional learning. It provides specific findings and guidance.

- Chapter 1 considers obstacles to equity and argues for a deep commitment to equity leading to personalized learning for students, continuous professional capacity building, leadership, and supporting systems development.
- Chapters 2, 3, 4, and 5 are four concise cases, showing school-based artifacts, processes, and approaches. As much as possible, the cases tell the story in educators' voices. Each case is accompanied by analysis that examines the lived values, specific professional learning practices, leadership, and systems we discovered as we visited schools and studied documents. Additional school artifacts are available online at the book website.
- Chapters 6, 7, and 8 reveal patterns across the four cases that have implications for professional capital building. Chapter 6 explains equity and supporting values that ground and shape professional learning. Chapter 7 names the fundamental form and practices of

professional learning required to personalize learning for every student. And Chapter 8 examines leadership and systems that facilitate sustainability and ongoing professional development.
- Chapter 9 provides a practical call to action to help you make the case for change.

WORKING ASSUMPTIONS WITH THE TEXT

The authors began with assumptions that schools making equity gains would show evidence of three themes:

1. Explicit commitment to equity, visible in school practices, that guides and shapes professional learning.

2. Job-embedded professional learning to support personalized student learning, emphasizing collaboration among multiple groups, with one or more knowledgeable professionals working at or with the school to help shape the program.

3. Leadership and systems that ensure continuous and sustained professional learning.

ABOUT THE FEATURED SCHOOLS

Each featured school's students have demonstrated overall gains and gains among students of color, students with special needs, and English Language Learners. The four schools are:

1. Stults Road Elementary School (preK–6), Richardson, Texas (Chapter 2);

2. Social Justice Humanitas Academy (grades 9–12), San Fernando, California (Chapter 3);

3. Montgomery Center School (preK–8), Montgomery Center, Vermont (Chapter 4); and

4. Tusculum View Elementary School (preK–5), Greeneville, Tennessee (Chapter 5).

Between 45% and 80% of students at the featured schools are from low-income families. In the two urban schools, over 90% of the students are African American, Hispanic, Native American, or Asian/Pacific

Islander. The two rural schools have primarily Caucasian student populations. Spanning regions across the country, two are urban and two are rural. Montgomery Center has 155 students across 10 grades while Stults Road has 525 across 7. We sought out diverse populations, sizes, and locations to identify both common and unique ways that professional learning would reveal itself.

Each of these schools is growing into equity and increasingly high achievement. While their journey is not complete, they have developed practices that recognize each student as a person and as a learner, and that use knowledge to provide individualized student challenge and support. This book shares their stories and their focus on professional capacity building to meet equity and excellence.

*The whole world, in Massachusetts, in China, should
have good teachers. Even sharks.*

—Matteo, age 7

Acknowledgments

Educators at the featured schools are making real what many consider impossible. We admire the energy, care, and expertise they bring to their work. We are grateful for their openness about triumphs and challenges alike, so that readers can learn from them. Their commitment and their trust in us made this book possible.

Montgomery Center K–8 Elementary School, Montgomery Center, Vermont

Social Justice Humanitas Academy, San Fernando, California

Stults Road Elementary School, Dallas, Texas

Tusculum View Elementary School, Greeneville, Tennessee

In particular, the leaders at the featured schools collaborated with us from start to finish. They helped ensure we had all the right meetings, interviews and data needed upfront, and later all the artifacts and details that bring the cases to life. Our special thanks to Darwin Spiller, Amber Leblond, Lin Wall, José Navarro, Samantha Siegeler, Jeff Austin, Beth O'Brien, Patricia Donaldson, and Stacy King. Thanks to district staff and partners who tracked down data and information that provided important context: Robinette Mitchell, Jennie Carey, and Jane Patterson. Three cheers for each of the teachers, administrators, and students interviewed, and to those we observed teaching and learning.

We visited additional school communities as part of our research. Thanks to educators at: E. Erik Jonsson Community School, Dallas; Cleveland Humanitas Magnet High School, Los Angeles; Boston Day and Evening Academy; and Camp Creek Elementary School, Greeneville, Tennessee. Their practice and wisdom also accompanied us on this journey.

Thanks to Stephanie Hirsh and Joellen Killion for offering wise counsel, leading advocacy, advancing research, and cultivating a regional and national community that makes us better persons and learners.

Susan Villani, Jill Berg, Victoria Duff, Mindy Kornhaber, Jan Phlegar, Mike Murphy, and Herbert Gleason were present to us at every stage of this effort with advice and affirmations that facilitated the next step. Leigh Peake, Jane Redmont, Linda Davin, Mariana Haynes, Berta Berriz, Betsy Drinan, and Susan Hayes were at the ready with just-in-time assistance. And our peer reviewers helped hone the final manuscript. Thanks to each and all of them.

We dwell in gratitude for key individuals who have shaped our learning and our work: John Cawthorne, Nelson Colón, Kathy Dunne, Steve Hamilton, Nick Hardy, Gerald Leader, Barbara Miller, Susan Mundry, Ewa Pytowska, Robert Sperber, Wendy Sauer, and Cheryl Williams. And thanks to colleagues across WestEd, Education Development Center, and *Success at the Core.*

Our understanding of learning, schools, and transformation has been enriched by educators in all the communities we have served. We are particularly grateful to these: Merrimack School District, Hooksett School District, Nashua School District, and Londonderry School District in New Hampshire; Syracuse City Schools; The Pike School; Russell Elementary, Mason Elementary, Ohrenberger, and Boston Teachers Union Pilot School in Boston; Central Park East Elementary School in New York; and Grace Academy in Hartford.

Arnis Burvikovs at Corwin recognized the potential for this book when he read Sonia's 2010 article on social justice and professional learning in *JSD*. He listened and guided deftly all along the way. Thanks to Veronica Stapleton Hooper, Terri Lee Paulsen, and all at Corwin who ensured a successful publication process, and to Emma Brett for elegant organization of data files.

Finally, we thank those whose leadership on social justice and change guided us personally as we developed this book: Cesar Chávez, Michael Fullan, Andy Hargreaves, Linda-Darling Hammond, Sonia Nieto, Jeannette Normandin, Ruth Rosenbaum, and Gloria White-Hammond.

It is our high and humble hope that this text honors the efforts of educators at the featured schools, and all who spend their days improving learning for every child they encounter. Their successes illustrate what all of us can and must accomplish.

NG: To the friends and family who supported me through this project—sharing sustenance, laughter, trouble-shooting, jigsaw puzzles, space, home movies, transportation, diversions, gardening support and walks in the woods—thank you. The joy you each bring to my life is immeasurable.

SCG: The love of extended family and friends from Boston, New York, Clifton, Putnam, Woodbourne Farm, Vancouver, Firenze, and Istria sustains me. Ongoing gratitude and love to David, for urging on what seemed a particularly poorly-timed project, for managing IT and family logistics with me at every turn, and for deftly helping pare down the manuscript to its essentials. Our sons propel me. Christopher's numinous stillness and Matteo's dazzling energy ensure that I consider new juggling moves, improve my chess game, and want all children to know joy and success.

PUBLISHER'S ACKNOWLEDGMENTS

Corwin gratefully acknowledges the contributions of the following reviewers:

Karen Brainard
NBCT, Teacher
Hilliard City School District
Hilliard, Ohio

David Callaway
Seventh-Grade Social Studies
Rocky Heights Middle School
Highlands Ranch, Colorado

Dr. Peter Dillon
Superintendent of Schools
Berkshire Hills Regional School District
Stockbridge, Massachusetts

Victoria Duff
Consultant
Learning Forward
Toms River, New Jersey

Dr. Melissa Kagle
Assistant Professor of Education
Colgate University
Hamilton, New York

Dr. Steve Knobl
High School Principal and Adjunct Professor

Pasco County Schools & Saint Leo University
Gulf High School
New Port Richey, Florida

Nancy Love
Corwin Author, Program Director
Research for Better Teaching
Acton, Massachusetts

J-Petrina McCarty-Puhl
Secondary Science Forensic Educator
Robert McQueen High School
Reno, Nevada

Ernie Rambo
History Teacher
Johnson Jr. High School
Las Vegas, Nevada

About the Authors

Sonia Caus Gleason (pictured right) has over 25 years of commitment to social justice and high performance within and beyond public education, particularly in communities with underserved populations. Her work includes consulting and coaching that raises student achievement; building community to sustain school and district innovation; developing effective partnerships that leverage reform; and designing and delivering research-based, professional learning experiences. Sonia has coached schools and districts around the country, and has supported cadres of coaches and facilitators in building capacity and navigating change processes.

As founding developer of award-winning *Success at the Core* (www .successatthecore.com), Sonia develops online, video-driven professional learning materials that cultivate classroom and collaborative leadership practice, and manages strategic dissemination partnerships. Her writing has appeared in *Educational Leadership, JSD,* and other publications. For the Regional Educational Laboratory for the Northeast and Islands, Sonia co-authored *How Eight State Education Agencies in the Northeast and Islands Region Identify and Support Low-Performing Schools and Districts.* She holds a master of education in administration, planning, and social policy from Harvard Graduate School of Education and a bachelor of arts in Italian studies and international relations from Connecticut College.

Nancy Gerzon (pictured left) has been supporting school districts to improve learning outcomes for two decades. As a senior research associate for Learning Innovations at WestEd, Nancy provides technical assistance, professional development, and administrative coaching to support school improvement and reform in New England and New York.

Since 2007 Nancy has been the lead consultant on two state-level implementations of classroom formative assessment, in Rhode Island and New York. In these research-to-practice projects she led professional development and dialogue about formative assessment for state policy makers, regional professional development providers, district and school leaders, academic coaches, and classroom teachers. In these projects, Nancy served as a bridge between researchers and practitioners as she worked to ensure that the voices of classroom teachers were present in policy dialogue, and, that the voices of researchers were a part of school-level dialogue about teacher practice.

In her work with low-performing schools and districts, Nancy works with superintendents, principals, coaches, and teacher leaders in order to build internal capacity and to develop strategies for sustained improvement. In recent years she has focused on supporting teacher leaders to align standards, instruction, and assessment, and to use evidence of learning to guide instruction. Through sustained multiyear work, Nancy has helped numerous schools improve achievement and exit Program Improvement status.

Nancy's work is guided by an enduring interest in how educational systems support individual student and adult learning. She is passionate about helping schools and districts create systemic supports for teacher learning, effective teaming practices, helpful team facilitation, and supportive learning structures. Nancy has a bachelor of arts in psychology from Stony Brook University and a master of arts in human resources from Rivier College.

The Case for Professional Learning to Support Equity and Personalization

1

School communities can grow into equity and excellence through personalizing learning. The powerful school communities in the four cases shaping this book prove it. These four Title I schools attend to the individual needs of each student, and have demonstrated increased student achievement for underserved students over 5 to 10 years.

Equity combined with high standards is their driving force. Determined to meet the needs of each student, personalization takes hold, and learning for both students *and* adults becomes engaging and effective. Significant practice shifts provide adults with daily opportunities to focus their own learning, in support of each student's success. Leaders and systems keep the efforts focused, accountable, and sustainable.

EQUITY AND ITS IMPEDIMENTS

Equity requires fairness and justice, so students are challenged and supported to meet high standards regardless of their race, ethnicity, economic class, gender, language, or ability. This is the American Dream realized through public education: Anyone willing to work hard can make it. Here society generally, and education specifically, bear responsibility for enabling this concept. Historically we have paved the trails to equity with

Supreme Court cases, court orders, community organizing, and policies, as we continuously review what we should provide, how high we should reach, and who should be included.[1] Progress has been made, but continued, and in some cases worsening, inequity demands more. Current, national issues focus on high standards and college access for all students, opportunities for deep learning, formative assessment systems, and effective educators. These initiatives play out to differing effects in states and communities. Continued vigilance is required: There are no shortcuts to equity.

Focusing on the Needs of Every and All Students

In the age of No Child Left Behind (NCLB), achievement has meant thinking about expectations for all students—groups in aggregate. In terms of federal legislation, this was a first. It focused educators on support to NCLB demographic groups. At its best, it has generated research on and systemic practices for historically overlooked groups and their needs—important steps.

These groupings also have their limits. For example, while a school's demographic data may indicate that 45% of the students are Black, they may be

- children of middle-class, college-educated African Americans;
- newcomers from Haiti with some formal schooling;
- fourth-generation African Americans whose ancestors never knew school success; or
- children from Nigeria with no schooling who only speak a little-known dialect.

> **Underserved students** are likely to be
>
> - economically poor;
> - immigrants;
> - racial and ethnic minorities;
> - English Language Learners;
> - students with special needs;
> - students with areas of giftedness; or
> - some combination of the above.

These examples belie the tidiness of the federal demographic group "Black." Recognizing the multiplicity of variations within racial and other categories means attending to them in order to reverse low trends of graduation and achievement, particularly among the economically disadvantaged, English Language Learners, students with special needs, and Black and Hispanic youth. But if we focus singularly on racial groupings and their broad descriptors, we don't fully get to know who students are, or what will enable their achievement (Conchas, 2001; Conchas & Noguera, 2004; Conchas & Pérez, 2003).

High achievement and equity means attending to *each student*.[2] This is different from thinking about students in aggregate, the *"all students"* framework, and puts an emphasis on students' individual gifts and needs. Each one counts and merits challenge and care.

Equity Commitments as Aspirational or Limited

Most educators and school communities have and believe statements about achievement for all. Yet these statements can remain aspirational, like many an unfulfilled New Year's resolution or wishes for world peace. They are held dear in concept but are not realistically planned for or actualized over the long term. School meeting agendas, instructional plans, and professional learning days may be perpetually one or two steps away from directly focusing on equity. In the end, it is expected and acceptable that only some students do well (Hilliard, 1991).

Goals can be too low, or too narrowly defined, to accomplish high achievement for all. Political pressure and policy goals may focus disproportionately on test scores. This approach may improve overall scores without fundamentally improving student learning. At best, the efforts chip away at equity issues.

Institutional Racism, Cultural Bias, and Cultural Blindness

Individuals, schools, and systems—either actively or passively—make exceptions to the idea that all students can learn.[3] When biases are systemic, they exclude groups from getting access to and appropriate support for learning.[4] For example, a new national K–12 study shows that male Black and Latino students are suspended at rates much higher than other groups (Losen & Gillespie, 2012). Subsequently, they are more likely to be expelled, drop out, and decide that school is not for them.

All students may be treated the same, though socioeconomics, race, language, and/or culture may vary. This blindness[5] can never get us to equity because everyone simply does not need the same supports and opportunities to learn. The reasons behind these systemic biases and discriminations continue to be debated vigorously.[6] In the meantime, individual schools and the nation writ large continue to work on narrowing achievement gaps that reveal inadequate achievement of the underserved, and an American Dream that remains unfulfilled for many.

AN EQUITY FOCUS LEADS TO PERSONALIZING LEARNING FOR EVERY STUDENT

A commitment to equity and excellence means recognizing that every child is a complex and compelling story, as a person and a learner. Part of educators' work is to uncover gifts. This does not negate federal groupings or working on equity in more targeted ways; it just acknowledges that they do not suffice.

Understand Students as Persons and as Learners

To meet each student where they are, they need to be understood as persons and as learners. This means recognizing the fullness of their gifts; their passions; their race, class, and culture; additional aspects of context and history; their families; their beliefs and values; and their possibilities.

There is also understanding students as learners. Learning begins with who students are and what they already know. The teacher is responsible for extending and deepening learning from that point (National Research Council, 2001). Sometimes, underserved students present extraordinary gifts and needs simultaneously:

- Anna, a Cape Verdean newcomer, is three years beyond her peers in science skills and knowledge. She arrives completely new to the English language.
- Ewa, a Polish American, is having difficulty communicating orally. Literacy diagnostics don't indicate a language problem. She's a great painter. When her teacher probes, she learns that Ewa's only parent is deaf; Ewa does not talk much at home. She signs.
- Alejandro, a second-generation Mexican American, speaks English, is a natural at soccer, and works hard at his studies. His teacher is challenged to figure out the source of Alejandro's difficulty in math.

Personalization

Understanding each student as a person and learner inevitably personalizes learning. The literature on personalization, starting with Theodore Sizer's (1999) work, points to personalization facilitating strong relationships between teachers and high school students. Teachers need freedoms and supports to understand students and personalize learning. In high school they need teaching loads that allow time to form meaningful relationships with students, (Yonezawa, McClure, &

Jones, 2012). Linda Darling-Hammond summarizes personalization this way:

> Schools' efforts to ensure that students are well known include the construction of small learning communities; continuous, long-term relationships between adults and students; advisory systems that systematically organize counseling, academic supports, and family connections; and small class sizes and reduced pupil loads for teachers that allow them to care effectively for students. (Darling-Hammond, 2010, p. 246)

Personalizing education can also reveal itself through acts of instruction and assessment. Learning begins with who students are and what they know; the teacher is responsible for extending and deepening learning from that point (National Research Council, 2001). John Hattie's (2012) description of effective teaching and learning requires that teachers know each student's current academic achievement, and are poised to attend to each student's next steps in learning.

> Teachers need to be aware of what each and every student in their class is thinking and what they know, be able to construct meaning and meaningful experiences in light of this knowledge of the students, and have proficient knowledge and understanding of their subject content so that they can provide meaningful and appropriate feedback such that each student moves progressively through the curriculum levels. (p. 18)

Within these relationships, daily practices focus on understanding students as persons and learners, knowing that as they change and grow, their learning itself changes over time. This involves teachers having deep knowledge of content, an understanding of what students are expected to learn in previous and subsequent grades, and abilities to effectively capture current student knowledge in assessments.

In *Growing into Equity*, the definition of **personalization** **includes both personal relationships with students, and classroom practices and multiple supports that recognize and attend to individual student gifts, circumstances, and needs.**

Personalization Happening for Some

There are individual teachers who understand and attend to every learner. In June, every child leaves these classrooms inspired, and often having made more than a year's progress. These are often the exception, rather than the norm.

Most educators and schools personalize in limited ways for students generally, and perhaps deeply for *some* students. They may be particularly low and high achievers, with extreme or obvious gifts and needs. And there are many, many teachers trying to figure out how students between these extremes learn. As professional developers working with educators around the country, the authors experience many teachers who feel hamstrung by circumstances, capacity, policies, bureaucracy, time, and limited resources. These educators are unclear about how to have an impact that reaches each student.

PERSONALIZING LEARNING FOR EVERY STUDENT REQUIRES REFRAMING PROFESSIONAL LEARNING

A commitment to equity is a quest for every student doing well and means systemic personalization. Successfully doing this requires continuously building educator skills, knowledge, and dispositions in and outside the classroom—ongoing professional learning.

The definition of professional learning proposed in the current Elementary and Secondary Education Act (ESEA) reauthorization,[7] and the consensus of national educational associations convened by Learning Forward, describes preK–12 professional learning as collective responsibility to provide a comprehensive, sustained, and intensive approach to raising student achievement.

1. It aligns with rigorous academic achievement standards and local improvement goals.

2. It takes place among educators at school and is facilitated by well-prepared leaders.

3. It primarily occurs several times per week among established teams to promote a continuous cycle of improvement (Hirsh, 2009).

Ensuring appropriate time and quality for professional learning is essential. Educators need to support one another to advance learning goals for individual students and themselves. Focused, ambitious goals are not just the result of working in isolation. Educators need to support one another, collaborate in various groups, and make effective decisions regarding student and school improvement. As they work individually, in teams and schoolwide, educators generate professional capital (Hargreaves & Fullan, 2012). This is not a nicety. It is essential to an aggressive equity agenda. Equity focuses and intensifies professional learning. It demands that professional learning create systematic space and scaffolding to learn and discern how students are unique as persons and as learners, and uncover individual students' instructional and other needs. Figure 1.1 on the next page offers an example of how one school with a fierce equity agenda engages professional learning experiences to support personalized learning through differentiation and integrating technology, with educators and students both advancing the cause.

LEADERSHIP AND SUPPORTIVE SYSTEMS ENABLE AN EQUITY AGENDA AND PERSONALIZATION

Advancing Equity With Professional Learning

Equity and Supporting Values
Focus and drive daily practices

Personalized Learning for Educators
Facilitates individual student success

Leadership and Systems
Sustain and guide continuous improvement

The example in the box above is a reminder that deep adult and student learning does not happen haphazardly. Research shows that next to instruction, school leadership is the second most important factor in improving achievement (see Hallinger & Heck, 1996; Leithwood & Jantzi, 2000; Leithwood, Louis, Anderson, & Wahlstrom, 2004). It defines leadership as having two essential functions: "providing direction" and "exercising influence." (Leithwood & Jantzi, 2000 p. 20). Increasingly, leadership functions are distributed. There's not one leader, but the web of leaders, followers, and their situations that shapes leadership practices (Spillane & Diamond, 2007). And there is evidence that sustained leadership over time allows for deep innovation to take hold.[8]

Figure 1.1 Personalizing Educator Learning to Advance Equity

Picture This: Personalizing Learning to Grow Equity Shapes Professional Learning, Leadership, and Systems

Stults Road Elementary's Mr. Campbell is part of the school's "21st Century Learning Cadre." This PLC is working on and disseminating instructional technology tools, and Mr. Campbell is one of several teachers on the team who is refining new strategies in his classroom prior to introducing them schoolwide. "His classroom is set up like a movie theater," says Lin Wall, Instructional Data Coach. Using his iPad and smart board, with a program called Pollster.com, he has developed formative assessment questions to begin a unit, and he will use this data to set up differentiated groups. In this "bring your own device" classroom, students use their cell phones to mark their answers, and the responses appear immediately on the smart board. "Mr. Campbell knows how to use this information to differentiate instruction" says Crystal Adindu, Literacy Coach. "He is willing to change what he is doing in the moment. He is ready to make instructional adjustments" right away.

Ms. Jaramillo in the third grade is exploring technology to differentiate and strengthen student engagement. In a recent writing lesson, she grouped students using multiple sources of data, including the results of the most recent writing assessment as well as multiple intelligences. Student groups work on the learning goal related to subject-predicate agreement. To provide peer feedback, students develop

---

Individual teacher with personal passion, sense of outcomes for all students, and connection to schoolwide goals develops expertise in the classroom, is an early adopter when it comes to integrating technology.

Team focuses on technology as a vehicle for achieving high outcomes for students, in sync with Mr. Campbell's passion.

Another teacher with passion and commitment to both technology and differentiation (as it relates to project-based learning), finds ways to personalize the learning within that framework.

Data Coach tracks individual teacher expertise and considers how to support Mr. Campbell's efforts.

Literacy Coach tracks how technology and literacy are integrated, and how technology is used to personalize instruction.

Students are given lots of opportunities to reflect on their learning, here using peer assessment. Technology helps teachers and students reflect on progress and explore next steps in learning.

There are whole school meetings where PLCs gather in small groups, but also have schoolwide sharing, where teachers are expected to try out new practices and then bring their learnings back to the full group.

The district is supporting these teachers to learn how to differentiate instruction so they can support colleagues in subsequent years.

digital recordings of their written work, using an avatar they have created along with voice-recording software. Educators and students alike have the opportunity to listen to and comment on each student's written work, deepening engagement and reflection through the avatar voice program. Crystal Adindu reflects, "Ms. Jaramillo is able to use technology in a way that engages students in order to meet their different needs in all levels."

Through the new iCougars program, students are helping teach their peers and educators about technology. As digital natives, "It makes sense for the students to be there for the teachers," explains school principal Amber Leblond.

The Data Coach comments that Stults "now has teachers who are a little bit more experienced with technology, and using some of the software to process data in a more efficient way." Through a "teachers teaching teachers" PLC model, educators gather weekly to share practices and integrate them into their learning.

Students with passion and expertise for technology are supported to grow and share their expertise with peers and with educators who need support in using technology.

The 21st Century Learning Cadre tries out new instructional practices then helps build schoolwide capacity.

For equity and personalization to transcend the realm of a few, iconoclastic teachers, the activities of professional learning have to be led, calibrated, and organized according to goals and needs. These leaders at the school level, and leaders at broader district, state, and national levels, each have opportunities to shape practices, protocols, and systems that sustain the work and ensure it remains iterative. Leaders, and the systems they shape in collaboration, allow for continued building of professional capacity as student needs become better understood, and as they change.

DECIDING TO DEEPEN AN EQUITY FOCUS

Making substantial advances in an equity agenda does not happen by accident. Sometimes a critical number of educators across a school decide that they are going to reach each student in a school, even if it is hard, even if everyone has some bias or blindness, even if it has been the domain of just a couple of people or the focus has been on one or two demographic groups in the past. Even if frustrated about progress. Actually, in part, because of it. Growing into equity requires that educators commit to every student achieving at high levels, emphasizing opportunities for every student learning, and working intentionally on each student's individual gifts and needs. The realization may start as a revelation for one or more educators, in the way that certain moments sneak up on individuals and announce that things cannot go on as they have. Or it may be a case of equity and excellence pulling each other along over time, case by case, building momentum. The more dynamic the dialectic on equity practice becomes, the more inevitable the work of personalization. As it grows, the work shifts from having a system that primarily attends to one class learning, or groups learning, to a system that personalizes learning for all students.

However it starts, this shift in student learning demands a reframing of professional learning for individual educators, collaborative teams, and schools as a whole. To address a more complex understanding of each student learner, adult learners need a support system and collective expertise.

These opportunities exploit the idea of the "adjacent possible" (Johnson, 2010), where new knowledge and breakthroughs rarely come out of the blue, but are more likely to be at the edges of what is already understood and extend from there. In education now, there is a growing knowledge of how students learn, how data analysis can inform instructional improvement, and how to organize cultures and professional communities to be effective. It falls to us to reach to the edges of research, best practice, and our own experience and wisdom to take the next step—one that helps us teach more children with greater care and competence than we ever have before. The following stories of four school communities point the way.

NOTES

1. See Darling-Hammond (2010) for a comprehensive historical and national political analysis.

2. This distinction between "all" and "each" comes from a framework for systemic analysis when it was introduced as being done from the perspective of the economically poor. This analysis was developed by Dr. Ruth Rosenbaum of the Center for Reflection, Education and Action. See www.crea.org.

3. See Tatum, 2003, for a discussion of active and passive racism.

4. Nieto and Bode (2011) examine structural flaws in systems and how to address them at the classroom and school levels.

5. See hooks (1992) for discussion on blindness as it relates to race as "racial erasure."

6. Cross, Bazron, Dennis, and Isaacs (1989) offer the Cultural Proficiency Continuum as a framework for understanding responses to diversity from cultural destructiveness to cultural proficiency. For more recent work on Cultural Proficiency see Robins, Terrell, and Lindsey (2003).

7. The definition of professional learning as Proposed Amendments to Section 9101 (34) of the Elementary and Secondary Education Act as reauthorized by the No Child Left Behind Act of 2001. For the full definition, see http://learningforward .org/who-we-are/professional-learning-definition#.UCuSuI44yfQ

8. See Sharratt and Fullan (2009) and Hargreaves and Braun (2012) for a discussion on the role of school and district leadership in capacity building.

Part I

Learning in Action

Four School Communities

Know Them by Name, Know Them by Need

2

Stults Road Elementary School (PreK–6), Dallas, Texas

> *Your principal, Mr. Spiller... created this program because after watching you every day, he noticed something different in you.... He noticed that you have what it takes to be a great student, an upstanding young man and a leader here within Stults Road Elementary School. He saw something in you that you may not even see in yourself at the moment... but you will in time.*
>
> *Why you? You were chosen because you have what it takes. You have what it takes to do whatever in life you want to do. You have what it takes to be a great student... Basically, you have "it," but you might need a little help developing "it." Now, don't get caught up in the fact that someone thinks you need extra help. What we're really saying is that with a little extra help, you can do things you never even thought possible. We think you can be exactly what you have ever dreamed of being. We want to invest in you to help you reach that potential.*

Source: Darwin Spiller. Stults Road Elementary Boys' Mentoring Program brochure. Used with permission.

At Stults Road Elementary School (Stults Road), in a working-class, North Dallas neighborhood,[1] several educators noticed that their program to support good behavior was not working for a small group of African American and Latino boys. When educators looked closely at this group, they noticed these boys did not have enough positive male role models at home. Principal Darwin Spiller,[2] himself an African American man, worked with colleagues to shape a plan for these boys. He reached out to men of color in the community to become mentors. Months later, a parent volunteer who had been supported to build skills and become the school secretary, started a similar group for girls who needed extra supports. That's just how it works at Stults Road. Educators use evidence and good judgment to identify an impediment to learning, and then collaboratively shape a personalized response to student needs. Immediately.

Asked what they're going to be focusing on next year, the leaders say, "We have no idea." Instead of elaborate plans that map out hundreds of action steps, they have high goals all around for every student and educator, and assumptions that everyone will work toward them. They look for solutions and continuously apply themselves to learning new practices, and receive the tools, resources, and time to support learning and implementing solutions. Short-term data cycles help them take the next right step and track progress overall (see Figure 2.1).

In the school's spotless entryway, celebrations of the school's success reflect numerous and varied accomplishments. The walls are studded with accolades for school and individual teacher achievements, as well as photos of students and teachers, student work, and questions for students to ponder. Higher up, a sign heralds the school year's theme: "Know them by name. Know them by need." Children pass by wearing T-shirts that say "Distinguished Student."

IMMERSION IN THE CULTURE OF LEARNING

Crystal Adindu, a campus reading specialist, supports both students and teachers in improving practice. This morning she is coaching a first-year kindergarten teacher, Lauren Trostel. At last week's grade-level team meeting, the novice teacher shared that she wanted to learn more about Writer's Workshop. Another team member offered to model a lesson in the new teacher's classroom. Then she worked with Mrs. Adindu to set it up that week. Using Writer's Workshop, the seasoned teacher demonstrates student engagement techniques that involve movement and Motown: "Stop! In the Name of Love" is sung with new lyrics, "Stop! It's the end of the sentence." She models approaches to student management, and strategies to build academic vocabulary. The first-year teacher and the specialist observe together, sometimes conferring, sometimes taking detailed notes. Later that afternoon, the specialist meets with the first-year teacher to reflect on the observation and help plan the next writing lesson.

A more seasoned resource room teacher, also new to Stults Road, *receives the same variety of professional learning supports* during her first year at the school—opportunities to learn from her grade-level colleagues, cognitive coaching with a trained mentor, daily interactions with instructional specialists, and mailbox greetings from the school Social Committee. This is the Stults Road welcome to *all teachers.* "The range of supports we offer teachers new to the school models rigor and engagement as the norm. . . . It's not disrespect about what teachers do or do not know. It's reflection on practice . . . both regarding work with individual students and general instructional supports, and doing that in collaboration," comments Darwin Spiller, principal of the school for nine years.

Interdependent and Aligned Teams

In early October, the third-grade team is reviewing reading assessment data, as it does weekly. The school instructional and data specialist, Lin Wall, has prepared a summary document for each child that outlines current and past assessment

---

Stults Road Elementary

Demographics and Commendations

Number of Students: 524

Number Eligible for Free and Reduced-Price Lunch: 80%

Percentage of Limited English Proficient: 38%

Percentage of Special Education: 12%

Racial/Ethnic Percentages:

- Hispanic: 47%
- Black: 41%
- White: 5%
- Asian/Pacific Island: 4%
- Other: 3%

Sampling of Commendations

- National Title I Distinguished School
- National Demonstration Campus for PLC Implementation
- Texas Education Agency Exemplary School
- Featured in Learning Forward (NSDC) and Laureate/Walden University Professional Development Videos
- National AVID and TRIBES Trainers
- Elementary Administrator of the Year, 2007

---

results from formative, progress-monitoring, and benchmark data in every subject, so achievement results are easily available at a glance. At this week's meeting, teachers are reviewing current assessment results to place students into *targeted instruction groups.* Targeted instruction time in literacy takes place for 45 minutes daily to ensure that any student who needs it receives additional time to master agreed-upon learning outcomes. All classroom teachers and learning specialists divide up the students, so they work in small, fluid groups. "We support every teacher to work with every level," Lin Wall comments. "Each student has to know multiple teachers. That gives them a lot of people who care about their learning." That same day, the sixth-grade team shares assessment data. Working with Tonya Mitchell, a campus reading specialist, they group 65 students for targeted instruction. Data grounds the meeting, and teachers analyze academic and personal information about students and groups: who needs help with engagement; who has trouble with context clues; which high-interest, low reading level materials will appeal to boys in one group; which after-school tutoring strategies have most helped a specific group of English Language Learners. The reading specialist shares new research-based tools she acquired at a district meeting; some will support enrichment for students who have mastered the content. As the 45-minute meeting comes to a close, each teacher creates an action plan with learning goals and instructional resources for their targeted instruction group. (See online resources for materials used to plan targeted instruction.) In addition, Mrs. Mitchell completes a Team Feedback form and e-mails it to the principal, mentioning lingering issues regarding students and team needs.

Figure 2.1 Stults Road Elementary School's State Assessment of Knowledge and Skills (TAKS) 2006–2011 Whole School Results

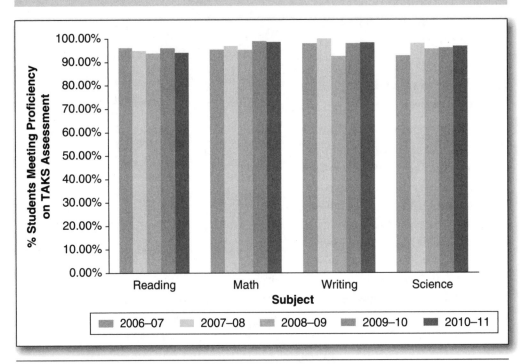

Source: Texas Education Agency, http://ritter.tea.state.tx.us/perfreport/aeis/2012/campus.srch.html (retrieved September 20, 2012).

As they take their leave, sixth-grade team members discuss this week's vertical team meetings, and one teacher offers a friendly reminder that the KN-6 Vertical Reading Team is developing challenging resources to support students in enrichment groups. Teachers developed these materials after analysis of grade 4–6 student assessment results showed that students who had met reading benchmark targets showed flat scores over time. Following an action-research model in which they review internal and external resources, vertical teams identified effective instructional practices for internal dissemination. The grade-level representative of the Vertical Reading Team promises to share the new enrichment strategies next week. This is newer territory as they work on helping students make good progress across time.

The next morning, the Instructional Leadership Team (ILT), comprised of the principal, assistant principal, instructional specialist, and two campus reading specialists, review the grade-level team meeting feedback forms. Their analysis guides next steps in learning for Stults Road teachers. Based on this week's grade-level and vertical team feedback forms, the ILT notes that teachers have begun discussing strategies for supporting higher-achieving students during targeted instruction and in the classroom. The ILT explores the idea of focusing Monday's weekly professional learning community (PLC) meeting on using enrichment strategies during targeted instruction, which will allow faculty to continue their work to implement new practices that are being reviewed by the vertical and grade-level teams. At Stults Road, PLCs have a unique characteristic, in that they are designed to build schoolwide capacity to implement evidence-based practice.

> **Thinkers and Texts That Influence Stults Road**
>
> - Roland Barth, Barbara Eason-Watkins, Michael Fullan, and Lawrence Lezotte, *On Common Ground: The Power of Professional Learning Communities* (2005)
> - Richard DuFour, Rebecca DuFour, Robert Eaker, and Gayle Karhanek, *Raising the Bar and Closing the Gap: Whatever It Takes* (2010)
> - Tom Dungy and Nathan Whitaker, *The Mentor Leader* (2010)
> - Stephanie Harvey and Anne Goudvis, *Strategies That Work: Teaching Comprehension to Enhance Understanding* (2000)
> - Joellen Killion and Patricia Roy, *Becoming a Learning School* (2009)
> - Ruby Payne, *A Framework for Understanding Poverty* (2005)
> - Teacher Leadership Exploratory Consortium, *Teacher Leader Model Standards* (2010)
> - Paul Tough, *Whatever It Takes: Geoffrey Canada's Quest to Change Harlem and America* (2009)

JUST-IN-TIME LEARNING FOR TEACHERS

Heidi Moore is a fourth-grade teacher who, during her first year, sought out support from various sources when classroom-level data did not indicate the degree of student progress she wanted to see. Mrs. Moore talks about how the opportunity to reflect on her practice and learn new skills helped her improve instruction and helped her students reach agreed-upon learning outcomes. "Last year, I got my second set of district math assessment results. I was panicking because I had a group that was not even close to passing the benchmark. I talked with my team, and I thought I needed even more than that. So I asked to talk with the assistant principal, Amber Leblond, and we came up with a plan. . . . I brought their grades up. All my kids met the benchmark." The plan was the result of analyzing data, finding error patterns, and looking at samples of student work. The heart of the plan had specific learning goals for the teacher, namely knowing how to create and manage small groups, how to ensure time for both review and for keeping pace with the curriculum. Mrs. Leblond made sure that Mrs. Moore had release time to observe successful lessons in this unit, view and reflect on a model lesson given by the instructional specialist, and participate in instructional coaching regarding her own lesson implementation. Principal Spiller reflects, "It just makes sense that if we offer different levels of supports for students, then why not provide them for teachers? . . . Part of the challenge is helping educators ask questions about their own practice. I want to provide a range of data and supports so they can attend to and drive their own learning."

A range of supports is available when teachers ask for them, and even if they don't. In one scenario, the ILT met and analyzed district benchmark data that showed significant low performance in one classroom. They reviewed the data in depth, and discussed current student and teacher needs in light of the findings. Since the classroom teacher did not self-identify as needing advice or support, the team moved into immediate action. They set up next steps for the reading specialist to observe the classroom and discuss the assessment results with the teacher. The ILT also identified a set of specific strategies for student support, including Lunch Buddies, use of Saturday school time (which is optional but can be recommended to families), and after-school tutoring. As Amber Leblond says, "At Stults, we turn the negatives into positives."

ANALYSIS

Over the past nine years, the Stults Road community has dramatically narrowed the achievement gap through changing structures, schedules, routines, practices, culture, and beliefs. This work has been led by a committed principal, a building leadership team, and a staff who share a steadfast commitment to equity. Schoolwide practices that they have implemented include eliminating tracking systems and revamping pull-out programs;

using weekly, short-cycle data for educational decision making and personalizing instruction; re-allocating instructional resources; establishing a responsive and nonpunitive discipline program as part of creating a caring climate; increasing rigor; extending learning time; establishing fluid and flexible student

> **Stults Road Elementary School Mission**
>
> At Stults Road Community we are committed to high expectations, appreciation of individuality, and encouragement of lifelong learners who will successfully function in today's global and culturally diverse society.

grouping strategies; and developing effective parent and community outreach programs.[3] They are coordinating and aligning efforts among individual student learning, and grade-level teams, the leadership team, and PLCs. They are moving into work on vertical alignment.

SCHOOL VALUES MADE EXPLICIT AND VISIBLE

It's all about learning. Learning is central to the work of everyone in the school building. People learn from analysis and reflection, from exploring research and best practice, and from trying out new ideas that may or may not be successful at first. Adults model the way, with their interactions setting the tone for students, and showing that real learning takes time, is nonlinear, and requires frequent reflection.

Success for underserved students, and those who educate them, is a given. The journey from *underperforming* to *award winning* at Stults Road has centered on a belief, shared now by most students, families, and faculty: All children can and will improve and achieve at high levels. "It is critical that we all believe that teaching all students and ensuring their success is a given," Principal Spiller asserts. A corollary is that all those who seek to support those students will also experience success. Many school awards confirm these values.

We can do more together than we can do alone. Collaboration is constant in small and large groups, among students and adults alike. It is the way that work of value gets done. This is a focused effort, with collaboration being coherent both within teams and across them, with many adults working together in many ways across the day, and with actionable observations and reflections resulting from undertaking shared work.

Relationships matter. The level and intensity of conversations about improvement reveal a high level of trust and care among educators, a school characteristic considered to be essential to school improvement (Bryk & Schneider, 2002; Noddings, 1992). As Lin Wall, instructional specialist, says about Stults Road, "Everything comes from relationships. . . . Continuous improvement of each educator and their ability to grow is the foundation."

Together, these values ground and focus the school community, and frame the resounding theme of the Stults Road case analysis: Ongoing, focused, and iterative professional learning for every educator leads to student success.

PROFESSIONAL LEARNING FOCUSES ON EACH STUDENT AS A PERSON AND A LEARNER

Understanding Student Behavior and Taking Action

The behavior model, for example, encourages children to explore alternative behaviors and provides intrinsic and extrinsic rewards when students are able to follow through with more appropriate behaviors. If an approach does not work as anticipated, teachers and school leaders analyze the data and then determine next steps to refine and deepen practices. For example, when analysis revealed that a group of older boys did not respond positively to the school behavioral model, the principal led the design of a new mentoring program (see introductory quote for this chapter). This supplemented the behavior model, which was effective for most of the students.

Collaboratively check on student learning and behavior every week. When students do well, and when they don't, it is first the charge of the teacher to figure out what his or her students' learning goals are, what will entice students to learn, and what to do when the work is too hard, too easy, or doesn't make sense.

With weekly frequency, teachers track on a range of behavioral indicators as well as academic ones. A range of data is developed, culled, and organized to help teachers understand findings, and focus on translating them into specifications for instruction and support (see Figure 2.2). Additional examples of student tracking forms are available in the supplemental online resources.

Data use, then, is focused on both student intervention (what does this child need next to be successful with this skill/content) and teacher intervention (what do we/I need to do next to be successful with these students, what do I need to learn to be more successful next week). As a daily practice, data drives the professional development necessary for every child to succeed. See Figure 2.3 as an example of how teachers document student academic needs for targeted intervention.

Figure 2.2 Kindergarten Personal and Social Development Report

Student _____

Six Week Period _____

Behavior or Habit	1	2	3	4	5	6
I show self-control by following classroom rules.						
I am responsible for my own behavior and actions.						
I share and cooperate with others.						
I respect myself and others.						
I accept and follow the teacher's directions.						
I clean up.						
I care for my classroom materials.						
I seek only my share of the teacher's attention.						
I can complete my work on time.						
I can work independently and use self-discipline.						

Rating Scale: Most of the time—3 Sometimes—2 Seldom—1

Parent Signatures:

Week 1 _____   Week 2 _____

Week 3 _____   Week 4 _____

Week 5 _____   Week 6 _____

Purpose of the Tool: This kindergarten inventory of behaviors is used to track a set of indicators weekly for student, teacher, and parent review.

Unique Use at Stults Road: This document is shared weekly with parents to facilitate sharing of feedback and conversations with parents and students in a timely manner. While these behaviors are commonly noted at schools, it is the weekly distribution to parents and the fidelity of use over time that makes this practice unique.

Source: Stults Road Elementary Instructional Leadership Team. Used with permission.

Figure 2.3 Targeted Instruction Three-Week Plan Overview

Teacher: Collaborative Teachers

Date: October 12th–14th

Group: Benchmark High Scorers

> Complete for each Targeted Instruction group

Students	DIBELS Information		Progress Monitoring	
			November 3	December 1
	DORF	Retell	Strategic	Strategic & Intensive
Student	160	88		
Student	108	37		
Student	121	54		
Student	90	51		
Student	108	39		
Student	115	Y		

Focus of Group

Week 1: Intro PROBES (Character Study/Traits)

Week 2: Intro Book Club (Cooperative Groups and Reading Comprehension)

Week 3: Continue Book Club discussions and start probing (stick-man, letter to character, advertisement for book/character, video advertisement)

Materials:
- PROBE Book, colored pencils, pencil
- class set of "Chocolate Fever" and/or "Ramona Quimby, Age 8"
- literature bookmarks, response journals

What's Next? Recommendations

Purpose of the Tool: This template displays reading assessment scores of students of a small, three-week, targeted instruction reading group. It captures individual strategies and interventions in the context of the group's goal.

Unique Use at Stults Road: The entire grade-level team makes recommendations about future practice.

Individual teachers track on progress of their small reading groups. Small-group reading strategies are determined by grade teams, and specialists use them regularly to track weekly progress. Note that low, medium, and high scorers all have small-group instruction.

Source: Stults Road Elementary Instructional Leadership Team. Used with permission.

Understanding Students Is Team Business

An individual teacher's first stop with questions about students is the grade-level team. This group, with both classroom teachers and specialists, acts as the brain trust regarding knowledge about students across the grade level. So while the individual teacher tracks evidence using Figure 2.3, it is the grade team that decides who will be in each small, changing, targeted instruction reading group every three weeks, and who recommends the instructional goals and strategies for each group. They also switch off, so teachers teach most or all of the students during the school year. And specialists who work with students for multiple years have a deeper knowledge of students over time. Teams and other adults who know the student and the community—bilingual, ESL, or special education teachers—may participate to share information about recent learning successes and challenges, current family needs, or other important personal concerns of a particular student. This deepens shared understanding to move learning forward and sets the stage for informal check-ins to follow up on specific children as needed.

The Instructional Leadership Team (ILT) is central in this work. As a whole, it makes sure that the schedules, data, and other resources are in play for this understanding of students to progress over time. It also moves in when it sees more global trends, as it did when it created the mentoring program for older boys. And as individuals, the principal, assistant principal, and specialists help teachers reflect on and understand their interests and needs, to take next steps in their own learning, in a range of contexts.

Understanding Students Is Everybody's Business

Building caring relationships and caring students translates into the importance of all the adults knowing and caring about all students in a variety of ways. Educators have increasingly been engaging families as partners in children's learning. Families and teachers now meet long before science fairs so families know how to support students working on their projects at home, so that everyone gets an equal chance at success. The idea for this meeting came from the school's Vertical Science Cadre. And this idea of collective caring and support is not just for educators and families: The year after the boys' community mentoring program started, the school secretary volunteered to organize a similar mentoring model for a group of girls. The attention to knowing and supporting students extends beyond the existing constructs; innovative ideas are sought out and welcomed.

The community-wide focus on understanding students also happens through intentional practices, including a shared responsibility for teaching all students across a grade level, collective analysis of student data, documenting and sharing students' successes, and all adults rotating dismissal and yard duties. This is no accident, but careful design that seeks to ensure students are known, appreciated, and helped by many adults in the school, the family, and the community.

Understanding and Encouraging the Adults as a Way to Understand and Educate the Students

It seems that an integral part of the work of having students understood at Stults Road is intrinsically understanding and encouraging the grown-ups who work with them. This was not a masterminded plan, as much as it started from "the gut." It made sense, and that has been building and becoming more formal over the years. Staff members throughout the school have been encouraged to develop their capacity, and have risen through the ranks over time, some from teacher to administrator, as both Principal Spiller and Assistant Principal Leblond have, but also those who started as volunteers or visitors and now hold a range of posts. Mr. Spiller, who has hired 93% of the current faculty over the past nine years, has a gift for seeking out and cultivating adults who share his high expectations and focus on equity and continuous improvement, and working with adults to develop their capacity. The talents, passions, and interests of adults are known and contribute to the life of the school in numerous ways. Teachers have multiple opportunities throughout the school year to demonstrate effective practices, participate in learning and apply new techniques and practices, and build their knowledge in an area of interest. Teachers are frequently tapped to lead new initiatives.

The adult learning is powerful modeling for students. Used to seeing a range of adults in the classroom helping each other, students are surrounded by images of learners in action as they, too, are invited to get excited about learning and the possibilities for growth that it brings. Both students and teachers are given opportunities in serious ways that include continuous cycles of inquiry, practice, reflection, and feedback. This makes for mirror images of student and adult learning in the school.

Students also witness parents being encouraged to learn. Several parents have been supported to take on different formal and informal jobs at the schools, and progressively climb the ranks, and courses are offered to parents in general to support their learning.

Professional learning is differentiated to meet the needs of all adult learners. Stults Road educators engage in a range of professional learning as it relates to their individual learning, team learning, and whole school learning (see Table 2.1). Each strategy and experience is planned with consideration to what's needed to improve teaching and learning immediately.

Table 2.1   Individual, Team, and Whole School Learning at Stults Road Elementary School

Individual Learning	Team Learning
Individual Learning Goals Teachers set individual learning goals each year, aligned with schoolwide improvement goals. *Coaching and Modeling* Teachers receive academic coaching when requested, or when student data indicates lower than expected performance on a specific learning outcome. *Peer Observations* Teachers are encouraged and supported to visit classrooms of colleagues to observe successful lessons (lessons that have shown good data-based evidence of improvement). Teachers frequently demonstrate model lessons in other classrooms, while a coach and teacher observe the home teachers' student learning. *Self-Initiated Learning* When teachers learn and hone new instructional strategies, there is a process for sharing across the school.	*Grade-Level Teams* Teams set SMART goals for team learning. Grade-level teams focus on data analysis and planning appropriate next steps for instruction for individual and small groups of students in targeted instruction. Teams provide weekly updates to the Instructional Leadership Team within 48 hours of meeting. *Vertical Teams* Content-based vertical teams develop articulated curriculum and work to deepen teacher content knowledge. Vertical content team meets every two to four weeks, or as needed; they are led by teachers. *PLCs* PLCs attend to common instructional issues raised by grade or vertical teams and/or the ILT over time; they are led by academic coaches, who bring data findings and support team dialogue related to data analysis and instructional actions. *Data Team* The Instructional Leadership Team (ILT) functions as a schoolwide data team. Benchmark data is charted by student and teacher. Teacher learning is, in part, driven by benchmark assessment results. ILT meets at least weekly, and responds immediately to team concerns and issues. *Scheduled Team Time* Grade teams meet at least 45 minutes weekly; PLCs meet weekly after school.

Whole School Learning

- Schoolwide meetings happen weekly. Schoolwide learning goals align with, complement, and frame ongoing professional learning done in grade-level and vertical teams.
- Weekly team meeting notes are reviewed from the perspective of whole school and individual teacher learning needs; such needs are most often addressed in whole school sessions.
- Successfully implemented action research findings are brought to whole school learning sessions for full-school implementation.
- Schoolwide book study groups focus on current research and practice.

LEADERSHIP AND SYSTEMS SUSTAIN EDUCATOR LEARNING

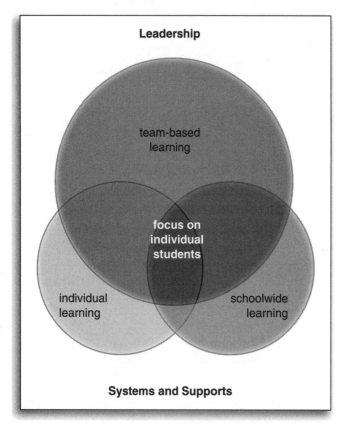

For continuous learning to take place, a complex system of practices, policies, and indicators are organized, layered, and negotiated on a daily basis. Many schools engage a range of the strategies that Stults Road has in place—small-group instruction, coaching, grade team meetings—but very few of them engage this many strategies with frequency and fidelity over time. And still fewer schools get to the place where the range of strategies relate to each other in a way that informs practice in such a public and shared way, freeing the principal from carrying this single-handedly. This is the place where Stults Road stands out, where they show how the ideal of continuous improvement takes form in a traditionally underserved community, and applies to individualizing learning for student and educators. It's useful to consider the aspects of the Stults Road systems in view of their continuity and ongoing self-reflection.

Immediate, continuous feedback loops. The ILT has an important role in this process, as it explicitly models how to employ data to make decisions. In *The Principal as Data-Driven Leader,* the authors name the primary challenge to the principal and school leadership team as showing "that almost every decision, whether large or small, immediate or strategic, is based on input of some kind, and most of that input is in the form of data" (Ontario Principals Council, 2009, p. 39). An expectation at Stults Road is that data will be used every day to inform key decisions and next steps in learning. Data forms the basis of schoolwide, team, and individual decisions, alongside academic decisions. As such, it is at the heart of the school's system of change. The ILT models data-driven decision making through the use of their feedback loop and through their daily practices of making (and communicating) data-based decisions. At Stults Road the data is compelling, current, and provides guidance that can be put to use, rather than being imposed by an external authority. Since data is analyzed both before and after new practices are implemented and new decisions are made, teachers provide ongoing input into the continuous feedback loop.

A critical component to the Stults Road professional learning model is the use of feedback to guide the work of the ILT and provide coherence to continuous learning (see Figure 2.4, Team Meeting Notes Template). Teams submit feedback forms to the principal, which are then analyzed, along with other data, to determine next steps for teacher learning. ILT data analysis might include review of survey data, behavioral data, observational data, or perceptual data from teachers, students, and families. Next steps in teacher learning might occur in whole group, small group, or individual configurations, depending on the data. ILT members review data continuously. Teacher team meetings are frequently designed to address emergent data trends. A significant body of research substantiates the role of this type of focused reflection in teachers' professional growth.[4]

In this way, the feedback loop at Stults Road becomes the mechanism through which leaders support coherence between individual, team, and organizational learning. Organizational development literature (Argyris, 1990; Argyris & Schön, 1978; Senge, 1990) notes that from ongoing, continuous reflection comes the capacity for individuals to align organizational and individual goals. The combination of continuous use of data, ongoing reflection, and interdependent teams allows for a systemic and coherent approach to support the primary organizational goal of addressing systemic inequities. Over nine years, Stults Road's evolving professional learning aligns with a growing body of research that shows high-performing schools have cultures that support ongoing teacher collaboration and professional inquiry.[5] And Stults Road is part of Learning Forward's network of Learning Schools, which provides professional learning supports and a community of like-minded schools.

Reflection: What are the continuous feedback loops like at your school? How easy is it to apply the feedback to inform practices or create new ones?

Figure 2.4 Team Meeting Notes Template

Team Feedback Sheet: Stults Road

Team: 5ᵗʰ Grade   Date: 9/12/2012

Team SMART Goal(s):

At least 85% of all student groups passing the Unit 2 Math Test.

At least 90% of all students reaching benchmark level for fall DIBELS testing (Dynamic Indicators of Basic Early Literacy Skills).

Team Members Present: Team Members Absent: (NONE)
                                          (include reason for absence)

Meeting Topics/Products/Outcomes:

Teachers will go over information in Goal folders with each student in their homeroom throughout the next week.

Curriculum Night Topics: Review DIBELS and benchmark criteria– explain expectations in all academic areas.

New plan for Targeted Instruction Groups

Differentiate instruction based on Math Unit 1 Assessment

Questions/Concerns from Team:

Request for counselor to work on conflict resolution/problem solving with students.

Administrator:

Purpose of the Tool: This tool guides quick, efficient note taking of team meetings.

Unique Use at Stults Road: Every team is responsible for submitting notes to the principal within a day of the weekly grade team meeting. The principal shares any issues of concern, or any issues that require attention, with members of the ILT. Supports or intervention take place within the week. It's the immediacy of response and fidelity of use over time that makes this resource effective in supporting professional learning.

Source: Stults Road Elementary Instructional Leadership Team. Used with permission.

An integrated set of varied research-based, non-negotiable, professional learning practices evolves over time. For example, the Stults Road case study articulates nearly all the elements outlined in the Learning Forward Definition of Professional Learning (Hirsh, 2009). The school has a comprehensive, sustained, and intensive team-based approach to learning that mostly occurs at the school in the context of the school day. At Stults Road, professional learning is led by internal leaders using current data to inform ongoing improvements to teaching and learning, and it is supported through coaching and opportunities to practice and transfer new skills. As outlined in Hayes Mizell's introduction to the Learning Forward Standards, Stults Road exemplifies the intent of the standards to have educators "thoroughly review performance data, establish learning goals, implement evidence-based learning strategies, and assess the effectiveness of their professional learning" (Learning Forward, 2011, p. 4).

At Stults Road, professional learning focused on helping students is intensive and non-negotiable. The unwavering expectation is that inequities are addressed immediately and that they are challenged directly, and in the moment. Professional learning and student outcomes go hand in hand. So whenever student learning data is not showing improvement, teachers must immediately identify what is not working. It is the teacher's responsibility to work within the system to make changes to ensure that strategies, approaches, and resources will be employed to improve the situation. What that means in practice is that adults must respond to achievement or behavioral data quickly, with encouragement and pressure to refine, revise, adapt, or deepen their instructional routines and practices. While the school culture motivates and empowers teachers and supports those who ask for help, when volunteered efforts are not sufficient, teachers receive targeted support to help resolve and address issues with additional guidance from instructional leaders. In this way, professional learning directly meets the needs of students who have traditionally been underserved.

This is in evidence in the description of newcomers to the teaching staff. The combination of high expectations, deep care for everyone in the building, intensive collaboration, and professional learning with a laser focus on achievement is new to most educators who first arrive to work at Stults Road. They receive both formal and informal mentoring and coaching that outlines clear expectations about the schoolwide practices, specific techniques, and specific student needs. Colleagues, specialists, coaches, and the administrators are all an intentional part of supporting the adjustment to the school. This range of supports is not just part of an orientation: It's the way teachers engage with one another all the time. (See Figure 2.5 for strategies used to integrate new teachers into the school.)

Reflection: What are the messages your school gives to newly hired staff? How might your practices reflect your community's aspirations and expectations? Which Stults Road strategies may be helpful in your community?

Interdependent teams. At Stults Road, the work of multiple, integrated, purposeful teams move learning forward in ways that support both individual and whole school learning. Providing professional development at the grade level and school level provides a base of understanding that leads teachers to support each other's improved practice (Darling-Hammond,

Figure 2.5 Strategies for Acclimating Stults Road Teachers to the School Culture

- Transparency about the goal to support every student making at least one year's progress, and organizing all resources and energies to achieve that end
- Clear information about the expertise in the school and expectations for student learning and professional learning
- Structured time for colleagues to offer demonstration lessons in the newcomer's classroom
- Coaching time that focuses on teacher questions, on observing specific students alongside the new teacher, on specific instructional practices that are a focus to the school community
- Expectations that teachers will call on specialists who focus on different content areas, as well as the principal and assistant principal
- Modeling in team meetings regarding data analysis and application to practice, collaboration in support of teaching specific children
- Structured reflection regarding teacher professional goal setting, as it relates to school priorities and individual student goals
- Invitations for new teachers to share a particular practice or expertise during professional learning sessions
- A Social Committee that provides a welcoming atmosphere; sends notes of encouragement during personal, tough times; and opportunities for the community to gather informally

Purpose of the Tool: This checklist offers a range of strategies to support the transition of teachers new to a school.

Unique Use at Stults Road: Leaders employ this range of strategies with intensity to make sure students are receiving the supports they need, to support teachers making the transition to a new community, and to demonstrate the expectations around collaboration to support individual students and teachers.

Wei, Andree, Richardson, & Orphanos, 2009). This type of collective work helps teachers take risks and solve problems to address existing issues in instructional practice (Ball & Cohen, 1999; Lieberman & Wood, 2002).

This plays out through five major team configurations at Stults Road, with each team tending to adult learning in service of students as part of their work. All educators participate in multiple weekly team meetings. *Grade teams* complete data review and work together weekly to plan next steps in instruction for individuals and groups. Figure 2.6 shows how small-group work is captured for each weekly Targeted Instruction group.

While grade teams are tracking and supporting progress weekly, K–6 *Vertical content teams* identify and address data-driven issues related to specific content, review grade-level expectations, and disseminate best practices.

Figure 2.6 Stults Road Targeted Instruction Week 1 Focus

This Week's Focus	Monday	Tuesday	Wednesday	Thursday	Friday
Group #1 Intro to PROBEing with Character Analysis	**Group #1** M:	**Group #1** M:	**Group #1** M:	**Group #1** M:	**Group #1** M:
Group #2 Intro to PROBEing with Character Analysis	G:	G:	G:	G:	G:
Group #3 Intro to PROBEing with Character Analysis	IP:	IP:	IP:	IP:	IP:
Teacher Notes: • Make sure to go over the rules for going and coming to Targeted Instruction time. • Talk about what will go on during this time.	**Group #2** M:	**Group #2** M:	**Group #2** M:	**Group #2** M:	**Group #2** M:
	G:	G:	G:	G:	G:
	IP:	IP:	IP:	IP:	IP:
	Group #3 M:	**Group #3** M:	**Group #3** M:	**Group #3** M:	**Group #3** M:
	G:	G:	G:	G:	G:
	IP:	IP:	IP:	IP:	IP:
Meeting the Needs of ALL students is not "extra" work . . . it is THE WORK!!!					

Purpose of the Tool: This template promotes communications across teams around learning goals and outcomes. It contextualizes the work in Figure 2.3.

Unique Use at Stults Road: After grade-level teams map out small-group work, this organizer tracks and makes public a week's focus, and clarifies the advice of three specialists as it relates to work with each group.

This form builds mutual understanding and accountability for the grade-level progress; it is updated and shared weekly.

M = Modeling
G = Guided Practice
IP = Independent Practice
TI = Targeted Instruction

Source: Stults Road Elementary Instructional Leadership Team. Used with permission.

In the example illustrated in Figure 2.7, the Vertical Reading Team studied the district reading data that revealed students meeting benchmarks were not making one year's worth of progress—and this was a stated school goal. Their analysis led to articulating SMART (Specific, Measureable, Attainable, Realistic, Time-bound) goals—as many teams do—for each grade level. Their work interfaces with the grade-level teams and the ILT.

Figure 2.7 SMART Goals From Vertical Reading Cadre

Stults Road Elementary School

Reading Vertical Cadre, Cycle of Continuous Improvement

Focus—Targeted Instruction for Benchmark Students

October 2011

SMART Goals for the Reading Vertical Team:

Kindergarten—90% of the benchmark students will reach a total of 15 more NWF (nonsense word fluency) in two weeks (by December 3).

First Grade—Increase the number of students achieving 20 words per minute by the next fluency assessment taken every two weeks to 90%.

Second Grade—Through literacy choices, the second-grade team will increase the percentage by 80% of benchmark students scoring a letter grade higher than the previous week on the weekly assessments.

Third Grade—95% of the benchmark students will score 90% and above on the next selection assessment.

Fourth Grade—The fourth-grade team will increase by 50% the number of students achieving a target score of 3 on short-answer questions on the weekly assessment over the next two full weeks by focusing on the skill of text evidence.

Fifth Grade—Benchmark students will be able to comprehend, infer, and make visual corrections, in relation to poetry written within a six-week period, by passing at commended levels on the January District Assessments.

Sixth Grade—Students will research a genre of literature to move them from simply recalling information to producing information and improving their scores on the Reading Profile so that 75% move from a 3 to a 4. The presentation can be delivered either on hard copy or electronically. This will be done in a two-week timeframe and will be assessed based on a teacher-created rubric, which focuses on research, organization, and presentation skills.

Purpose of the Tool: These are goals developed by the Vertical Reading Cadre, in response to data analysis revealing benchmark students were not advancing adequately.

Unique Use at Stults Road: When vertical cadres determine goals, cadre members from each grade take this information to the lead person on each grade-level team; the information is conveyed to grade levels. This is fed into the targeted instruction and other grade team work, and is considered alongside other data analysis. The ILT concurrently tracks on trends related to these benchmark students.

Source: Stults Road Elementary Instructional Leadership Team. Used with permission.

Professional learning teams research, explore, and share best practice related to schoolwide initiatives, such as behavioral planning and sharing new curriculum and instruction. *Vertical cadres* include instructional and noninstructional staff that organize and develop innovative approaches to campuswide events such as science fairs and literacy nights. And the ILT, referenced throughout the case and this analysis, is the constant, making sure that other teams are organized and supported to fulfill their charge, that the learnings of one group transfers to the next, and that new ideas are further developed.

> **Reflection:** At your school, how well and quickly are the efforts and needs of different teams communicated to the people who can support them? To one another?
>
> Are the teams working interdependently toward the same goal? Are there places where there are disconnects, or where they are competing?

Multiple leaders in play. Achievement is not something you attain, but consistently work at, with a constant press for analysis and reflection of next steps. At Stults Road, this is true of the principal, and increasingly true of the ILT, who embodies this commitment and plays it out in many ways, including sustaining professional learning. At the same time,

> If we want our schools to be laboratories of innovation able to tackle the significant challenges they face, school, leaders and teacher leaders must work together to identify, replicate, and scale up programs and practices deemed effective in supporting student learning. (Teacher Leadership Exploratory Consortium, 2010)

The ILT is drawing upon the Teacher Leader Model Standards to help the entire faculty reflect on their leadership in a variety of ways, and to think about how each teacher enlivens and guides systems that seek continuous learning and improvement.

Professional Learning Systems as Organic and Iterative, Flexible and Structured

At Stults Road the nature of the systems are as important as what they organize.

Organic and iterative. Ensuring a system of support for teachers must necessarily involve a range of pathways to increase teacher knowledge and skill. While schools begin this work through many different entry points, ultimately their journey includes ongoing and iterative professional learning practices that support faculty to work together to focus on meeting the needs of underserved students. At Stults Road, the systems of professional learning necessary to support personalization for all learners developed organically over time, through reflection and analysis that originated with the principal, and that grew to include teachers, the ILT, and district leaders. District staff are key resources in the work, naming issues, making data available, and providing key resources in timely ways. Iterative changes to their approach were developed based on examples from other successful schools, shared and ongoing review of research, and analysis of their own practice. Educators at Stults Road support continuous improvement through student inquiry, believing in the need for continued growth to foster ongoing dialogue, reflection, and action-research to deepen and improve instructional practices.

> **Reflection:** At your school, are the shared values shaping the practices and systems or are the systems the driver? Is the implementation of systems the goal, or are student outcomes the goal?

Flexible and structured. Professional learning is flexible in that the daily nature of it is grounded in solving current problems of practice, driven by individual teachers' learning goals, and bound in analysis of current data and trends. At the same time, professional learning is highly structured in that it takes place at specific team times each day, different groups have very specific charges, the flow and timing of different data shape cycles for analysis and reflection, high standards and frameworks guide the work, and varying tools regarding team and school performance are continuously infused into meetings to press for continuous improvement.

Together, these findings point to continuous, complex mechanisms that make for a reflective, yet fast-paced adult learning system. This includes mechanisms for reviewing data weekly and responding to findings immediately to ensure that not a moment of instructional time is wasted. The leadership team has also developed a mechanism to support teachers showcasing instructional practices that have yielded strong results; this happens both during and beyond the school day. Finally, the leaders also are developing skills of colleagues, parents, and volunteers, and finding ways to integrate those persons, with their new capacities, into the life of the school.

NOTES

1. For profile of the district, see: http://www.risd.org/group/aboutrisd/aboutrisd_main.html (retrieved December 16, 2012).

For school profile, see: http://www.edline.net/pages/Stults_Road_Elementary (retrieved December 16, 2012).

School data from http://ritter.tea.state.tx.us/perfreport/aeis/index.html. (retrieved September 20, 2012).

2. Darwin Spiller was principal at the onset of this study in October 2011, and Amber Leblond, who was assistant principal, became principal in June 2012.

3. See Kannapel, Clements, Taylor, and Hibpshman (2005); Ball and Cohen (1999); and Herman et al. (2008) for additional documentation on best practices in school reform.

4. For examples, see Constantino, De Lorenzo, and Kobrinkis (2002), Danielson and McGreal (2000), and Lambert (2003).

5. See Darling-Hammond and McLaughlin (1995); Robbins and Ramos-Pell (2010); Seashore Louis, Leithwood, Wahlstrom, and Anderson (2010); and Waters, Marzano, and McNulty (2003).

Students First 3

Social Justice Humanitas Academy (Grades 9–12), Los Angeles, California

> *Our goal for our students is not for them to merely be doctors, teachers, or lawyers, but rather doctors, teachers, or lawyers that change the world. By working for justice in education and teaching social justice to our students, in what we teach and how we teach it, we will empower our students to become the stewards of their own communities with the self-efficacy to fight for social justice for themselves and their communities.*
>
> *We believe our students are best empowered when the teachers at our school also feel empowered. This movement is a teacher led reform. Teachers, along with community partners, will be in charge of every aspect of this school from curriculum and instruction to budgeting. We ask, who better to make these decisions than the people closest to the students, the people who have dedicated their lives to the education of others?*

Source: Social Justice Humanitas Academy Elect-to-Work Agreement, 2010–2011. Used with permission.

The year 2012 may have been the single, worst[1] time to visit or to start a school in Los Angeles. While the Design Team planned a small school to ensure the centrality of relationships with students, state budget cuts resulted in high school student-teacher ratios averaging 35 or 40 to 1 (Kirst, 2011). Dust clumps in hallways bear witness to slashed custodial budgets. Nonetheless, the faculty at Social Justice Humanitas Academy (SJ Humanitas) was completing its first year as a pilot school in a new school building, the Cesar Chavez Learning Academies. Pilot schools are like district schools accountable for district outcomes and the same budgets, while they have autonomies regarding their curriculum, instruction, assessment, professional learning, hiring, and budget.[2] SJ Humanitas does not screen students for admissions and draws on students according to the district guidelines. It is in the Sylmar neighborhood of the Los Angeles Unified School District, where, "In our community, only 55% of the adults have high school diplomas, the per capita income is $15,374, and our hardworking students from hardworking families are in need of inspiration and opportunities."[3] But the educators are not starting from scratch. Their interdisciplinary instruction and intensive student support model was incubated for over 10 years as a small learning community (SLC) within the nearby, comprehensive Sylmar High School, which as a whole was historically low performing. There the Social Justice Humanitas Academy demonstrated that, with the right supports and challenge, students can be successful.

Most of the students from SLC at Sylmar made the physical move with the model, as did 8 of 20 teachers.

On Thursday afternoon, teachers are making last-minute preparations for the next morning's Very Important Person (VIP) meeting. What's a VIP meeting? Teacher leader Samantha Siegeler explains, "If a student is struggling in my class, I e-mail the student's other teachers to find out how he or she is doing." Patterns in behavior or performance that warrant further probing can catalyze a VIP meeting. All the student's teachers come together to meet with the student and his or her family member(s) about how to support the student's improvement. About 50 meetings will take place each year.

This integral practice in support of students is also an important act of teacher collaboration and learning. Teresa Tirado, 11th grade social studies

Social Justice Humanitas Academy

Demographics and Commendations

Number of Students: 460

Percentage Eligible for Free and Reduced-Price Lunch: 68%

Percentage of Limited English Proficient: 69%

Percentage of Special Education: 11%

Racial/Ethnic Percentages:

- Hispanic: 94.5%
- Black: 2.5%
- White: 2%
- Asian/Pacific Island: .5%
- American Indian: .5%

School Achievements: Designated as Los Angeles Unified School District (LAUSD) pilot school during first possible year, 2011–12

Teacher Achievements:

- Three National Board Certified Teachers
- 2009 California Teacher of the Year
- 2010 Special Education Teacher of the Year
- 2012 Facing History and Ourselves, Margot Stern Strom Teaching Award
- 2012 LAUSD Teacher of the Year

teacher new to the school and to high school teaching, explains that it's helpful,

> Being next to those individuals who are more experienced, who showed me the ropes of what I should be doing, how I should be asking the questions. Really focusing on the fact that individual students need some form of assistance and making sure that we are asking the questions to make sure we are getting the answers that we need to help him or her. For me it is always an eye opener, particularly when parents are open about what's going on and are willing and able to help us out in the success of their own child. And I really like to see when the students realize "Like wow. All my teachers are here. They really care about me."

This is one of the ways Ms. Tirado has absorbed the school's mantra, Students First. "And I definitely agree," she quickly adds. "It's a lot of work, but definitely worth it."

In addition to offering engaging and rigorous teaching, "Students First" means getting feedback from students on teaching twice yearly, helping them lead family conferences, ensuring a lot of individual student conferencing contextualized by five-week learning cycles, having student peer mentors sit in on IEP meetings to advocate for their mentees, and dedicating four hours weekly to advisory.

WE SEE THE HUMANITY IN THE STUDENT

Some schools dodge tougher or more troubled students by transferring them or letting them opt out of learning. Samantha Siegeler and Jeff Austin, lead teachers, coordinate professional learning and shape a range of practices. They talk about how their school is different, in that they are relentless in supporting students regardless of their circumstances. Mr. Austin explains:

> We just don't do that. . . . We'd rather see the kid just deal with their issues. Most of our kids who are acting up, there's a really good reason why they are acting up. And rather than pushing them away, which they are used to, we'd rather make them face it. "You know what. You've been in a gang for your whole life, now what?" . . . When a student finds out we are not going to kick them out, they figure, "I'd guess I'd just better do my work." . . .

We are going to keep on their case—in a positive way. Even Lupe[4] . . . He's so deep in the gang life. He may get killed. . . . He's got the three strikes: gangs, drugs, fighting.

Ms. Siegeler extends Mr. Austin's thought:

Even in those situations [Lupe's situation], we see the humanity in the student. Because a lot of schools would stick him in the office and be done with his education. But he goes to every class every day. . . . On Tuesday, he was having a personal problem. He's empowered enough to know he can come into the office, ask the counselor, "May I please have my work and do it in the office?" He completed his work and sent it back up to me. . . . At a meeting he told us it was the first time teachers ever checked out books to him.

Challenge and support is also there for Rosalinda Mendez, a ninth-grader: "We matter as a person not only as a student. . . . You have to think deeply here." Rosalinda talks about how she e-mails her completed assignments to teachers, because that's how it's done in college. She shares her Geography Interactive Notebook, whose cover has a collage of magazine cuttings. "This one is a white tiger. I picked it because it is unique. The lion I picked because it has power." The class probes into issues of identity, the geography of life across time, "not only Earth. . . . It's not just geography. It's about respecting each other, loving each other, so you won't lose your humbleness. . . . It's about consumption and how it affects our country and the world." Like most of her peers, Rosalinda will be the first in her Mexican American family to go to college. She's thinking about studying psychology at Stanford. "I want to be able to help my family."

How do you provide teacher learning that supports seeing the humanity in others? One way is that students and teachers take up founding principal José Navarro's Weekly Challenges, opportunities for specific acts of kindness across the community. Mr. Austin elaborates, "It is also about personal growth and the realization of the impact that kindness can have on those around you." Several mention the annual, three-day, summer retreat as an important time for reflection on these bigger issues. Mr. Navarro offered a homework assignment called "A Leadership Metaphor," where teachers talked about their personal journeys to becoming teachers and leaders at the school. Ms. Siegeler described her experience: "I learned things that I had never known. At the very end of it we were crying our eyes out. A lot of us were talking about our academic struggles, our personal struggles." Why so personal? Mr. Navarro explains:

It was letting them experience what kids experience. We have humanized ourselves in the eyes of each other. You are going to remember this when X forgets to give you a paper on time or when they send a student late to your classroom—those little things that can let us snap at each other. "I'm going to remember that X is a human being. You are not just the teacher two doors down." And that act of humanizing each other and humanizing ourselves creates the relationships that allow us to interact in a certain way. And we ask our students to give of themselves so they can humanize themselves in the eyes of everyone, including their teachers. We ask our teachers to do this with students on the first day. You have to give of yourself if you want these students to acknowledge you and to learn from you. So that's part of the retreat.

Building understanding develops relationships, which is especially important when the work is hard and the goals need to be held in common. It also facilitates meeting people where they are.

RIGOR ALONGSIDE RELATIONSHIPS

Relationships are an important starting point here. So is rigor. All students are on the college-prep track—no exceptions. Students receive feedback daily and weekly, and benchmark data every five weeks. It all relates to the school's own standard: Are you on track to be able to go to and through a good college? "Across Los Angeles Unified District, 30% of the students graduate having successfully completed the courses needed to enter California State University (CSU) or University of California (UC) system. At our school last year, it was 85%," reports Mr. Navarro (see additional data in Tables 3.1 and 3.2).

Students understand this long-term, college-readiness goal upon arrival, and the idea is reinforced by the depth and range of work and feedback, through college visits, and in posting seniors' photos in the hall alongside the name of the college they'll attend. Using multiple measures, student performance is ranked as gold, silver, bronze, or red. Gold and silver means performance is in range to get into the University of California system. Bronze performance qualifies for California State University admission. This is how Ms. Siegeler explains red to students: "You do not qualify for a four-year college. This is an issue. We need to stop and re-evaluate and offer you more support."

College is a major divergence from family tradition for most students, and teachers are conscious of creating an emotional and intellectual bridge to get them there. Mr. Navarro explains, "There's a priority here to

Table 3.1 California High School Exit Exam First-Time Pass Rates–California, Social Justice Humanitas Academy, and LA Unified—2012 Results

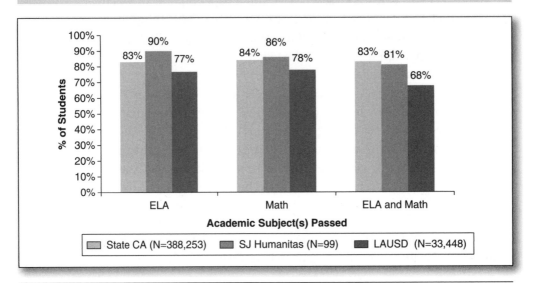

Source: California Department of Education, http://dq.cde.ca.gov/dataquest/cahsee/ExitProg1 .asp?cLevel=State&cYear=2011-12&cChoice=ExitProg1&cAdmin=C&tDate=000000&TestType=E&c Grade=10&Pageno=1 (retrieved on December 1,2012).

Table 3.2 2011–2012 High School Performance Metrics

Goals and Metrics	Los Angeles Unified School District Results (2011–2012)	Social Justice Humanitas Academy Results (2011–2012)
Four-Year Cohort Graduation (percentage of students graduate in four years)	64%	92%
Students on Track to Meet State University Course (a-g) Requirements	34%	50%
Instructional Days Lost to Student Suspension	26,287	2

Source: Los Angeles Educational Partnership, 2012.

understand students for who they are, and be relevant to them based on that understanding." He has asked his students,

> "How many of you kids have seen someone die, with your own eyes?" They all raised their hands. "How many of you were holding them when they died?" About half raise their hands. Our kids have a very acute sense of their mortality. That's why you need relevance. They are offended when we waste their time.

INTERDISCIPLINARY LEARNING FOR
STUDENTS AND TEACHERS

At SJ Humanitas, interdisciplinary learning is fundamental to make learning relevant, engaging, and challenging. Tim Knipe, 11th grade English teacher, lead teacher for the 11th grade team, and part of the school's Design Team that developed the pilot model, describes it this way:

> When you come to the school you sign an agreement that says that's the way you are going to operate in the classroom. . . . The lessons are constructed together. In traditional education you have teachers creating lessons more on a vertical basis. So the kids are in this world of English and then they go to a world of geography. What happens here, I liken it to an immersion in a foreign language. Listen to a language being spoken. Watch it being applied. Listen to inflection, nuance. The same is true for any individual discipline. If you are trying to learn English, you want to see it applied. It's not good enough to talk about syntax and grammar. You need to see it applied in your history book. There's no learning if it is not applied.

This month, students are immersed in studying the Holocaust. In Mr. Knipe's class, students find a set of concentric circles on the board. He prompts them to talk about who is in their inner circle, the people who matter most. He presses them to put the people in their lives into a hierarchy, to think about how easy it is for some people to be seen as "other." They are reading *Maus*, Art Spiegelman's graphic text about his father as a Polish Jew and Holocaust survivor. Mr. Knipe explains:

> They have interviewed a family member who has been part of a social injustice. They had to write about it in a narrative, including themselves in a framed narrative. And they are developing a graphic novel, following the model of *Maus*. . . . It has been a real eye-opener to them to understand, "My mother went through this, so that's why she does that."

In Genetics down the hall, paired students ponder dominant and recessive genes as they consider their facial features and what genetic comingling would produce. The theme harkens back to racial purity, and who is "other." Teresa Tirado reflects: "It [interdisciplinary learning] allows for the kids to make more connections. I remember one of my students saying, "I really like that . . . we are learning with you, Mr. Knipe, and Ms. Evans. It helps me understand."

When doing curriculum planning, Ms. Tirado talks about a balance of thinking things on her own, with others across the school who teach history or government in other grades, and primarily with her grade team colleagues, especially Mr. Knipe. "I don't know what I would have done without him. . . . For the whole team, he has been our glue, showing us how this model really works, and how to be successful."

Mr. Knipe also relies on colleagues:

[It's] the support that we give each other within the team . . . the time that we spend in grade-level meetings, which is built into the day. We have one-half hour every day before the first period during the day, for whatever we want to do: share materials, get feedback. . . . Many of us are here before then. We get a lot done.

When Mr. Knipe needs help, "I go to other teachers if there are specific things or they don't work. We, as a group, are very keen on observing each other, so that we can get feedback on our practice."

Mr. Navarro comments on the interdisciplinary model:

You can't move forward without the team, so it is a form of peer review. . . . Units of study are mapped together, then the teachers assess together, which keeps them accountable. So that's a way of doing peer review on content.

Learning with external partners. While the grade teams are primary, Mr. Knipe is quick to mention, "We also have important partners, the first one being LAEP." The Los Angeles Educational Partnership (LAEP) is the nonprofit that brokers a range of community partners

Thinkers and Texts That Influence SJ Humanitas

- Grant Wiggins and Jay McTighe, *Understanding by Design* (2005)
- Howard Gardner, *Frames of Mind: The Theories of Multiple Intelligences* (2000)
- Linda Darling-Hammond and John Bransford (Eds.), *Preparing Teachers for a Changing World: What Teachers Should Learn and Be Able to Do* (2005)
- Jeanne Oakes and Martin Lipton, *Teaching to Change the World* (2003)
- Fred Newmann, *Authentic Instruction: Restructuring Schools for Intellectual Quality* (1996)
- Theodore Sizer, *Horace's Compromise: The Dilemma of the American High School* (1984)
- Carol Ann Tomlinson and James M. Cooper, *An Educator's Guide to Differentiating Instruction* (2006)

and supports the Humanitas interdisciplinary model they founded in 1982.

There is a second, key professional learning partner: The *Maus* lesson came from Facing History and Ourselves resources. This organization offers curriculum resources and opportunities for teachers to reflect on ideas related to community and injustice, starting with the Holocaust, and what it means for thinking and action today. "For Facing History [professional learning] we have one Friday a month, so I [Mr. Knipe] set that up. Someone comes in and gives a workshop on an issue. At the beginning of the year we develop the list of issues based on seminars that they provide."

Social justice for teachers, too. The interdisciplinary model and student supports, alongside development of a democratically run school, is a tall order. This is especially so since the shift of buildings and becoming a pilot school resulted in numerous teaching positions opening up. This required a critical mass of new teachers to learn the ropes quickly. While the start-up work will wane, Mr. Navarro knows there need to be systems to sustain teacher leadership and learning:

> I realized this social justice issue we were having, that it wasn't just students. . . . It was also our teachers. It has to do with [teachers continuously having to make] these Herculean efforts. They weren't built that way. The schools weren't built that way. . . . If you want sustainable change, you have to build capacity. . . . It can't be just simply sacrificing your life for students. . . . There has to be a way to empower the teachers so they feel they can make these changes. . . . You have to hold them accountable. You have to give them real power. You have to pay them.

Mr. Navarro believes systems for professional learning are central to social justice for teachers. During a visit to Japan, which he visited as California Teacher of the Year, he observed a model where teachers taught for half the day, and then planned and reflected the other half. It inspired analysis:

> We developed a matrix, and most of our teachers have two conference periods for planning/professional development (100 minutes) in a six-day cycle. . . . I want to move to the Japanese model, so I'm inching my way there. What does the time provide? A space where you can bring what you need to talk about to help students.

Another important concept grounds teams and faculty collaboration in general. "When you're creating these laboratories of democracy, people are going to be wrong, and they need space where they can be wrong, be human and be forgiven," explains Mr. Navarro.

Anything worth doing is going to be hard. This school draws a set of teachers who are entrepreneurial and drawn to advancing social justice. Mr. Navarro observes that the core group of teachers likes the Humanitas model, and the commitment to understanding each student and helping them excel.

> It's labor intensive. Most who have been around the block know that the grass isn't greener. Sure you can go somewhere else, but you're beating your head against a wall, dealing with deans, you're dealing with a lot of discipline issues. Discipline is the one thing we just don't talk about. It's such a small part of what we do because of the restorative justice model we use. It is very clear to our kids that we care about them. A lot of things that drive you crazy here are more like curriculum, dealing with other adults, [who can be] a pain in the ass. . . . You are going to be tired at the end of the day. What kind of tired do you want to be?

Mr. Knipe is one of the teachers who stuck with the model over six years. As the model evolved within a larger, comprehensive high school,

> We used to get crap from other teachers [for working so hard]. But the harder I worked the better it was in the classroom, so I just kept working that hard because I wanted it to become easier in the classroom. So this was a natural progression. The reason I'm still here is that it seems to work, and we are making a difference. Anything worth doing is going to be hard.

ANALYSIS

Social Justice Humanitas Academy is a spirited urban high school in its first year as a small school, after a decade of building up leadership, curriculum, and capacity as an SLC. They are working to demonstrate that rigor, a social justice focus, and personalizing are not incompatible. They actually can and do reinforce one another. The school's commitment to learning is in evidence through joint efforts of teachers to support each student being ready to succeed and lead in college, the culture of observation among teachers, and the continuous pursuit of social justice through personal and academic engagement of students.

SJ Humanitas has a range of values statements and documents developed over time (see Figure 3.1, Mission and Vision Statement, Figure 3.6, Humanitas Elect-to-Work Agreement, and the Habits of Mind document in the online resources) that reveal clear beliefs.

Figure 3.1 Social Justice Humanitas Academy Mission and Vision

Vision

Our vision is to achieve Social Justice through the development of the complete individual. In doing so we will increase our students' social capital and their humanity, while we create a school worthy of our children.

Social Justice Humanitas Mission

The mission of the Social Justice Humanitas Academy is:

- To make intelligence and character the goal of education.
- To build our students' resumes as well as their characters.
- To create an academically rigorous, relevant, and safe learning environment for all students.
- To teach the state standards and the life lessons behind them.
- To create a student-centered school in which all stakeholders, parents, teachers, and community members are responsible and accountable for our students' success.
- To leverage the resources of our community to create a college-going environment so our students can get to and through college.
- To create a holistic and collaborative model of instruction and management to develop all of our students' talents to their fullest.
- To challenge our students and create mechanisms to support them in meeting that challenge.
- To foster the development of civic minded individuals who choose to participate and who see the greater good as their good.
- To have our students gain compassion, feel empathy, understand rather than simply judge, and develop the ability to apply their knowledge in diverse settings.

Source: Social Justice Humanitas Academy Mission and Vision Statement. Used with permission.

SCHOOL VALUES MADE EXPLICIT AND VISIBLE

Social justice. The commitment to social justice permeates school practices. Students traditionally on the margins receive opportunities and supports often only afforded to those of means, and all the students who cross the school's threshold are supported to be college-ready and to be leaders in the society.

This idea maps onto the literature on multicultural education.[5] Taken to the next level, it also seeks to model a socially just community in classrooms (Nieto, 2010). At SJ Humanitas Academy, because they believe in that fundamental premise of all good English teachers, "show, don't tell," teachers strive to model these values in order to teach the concept to students.

Multiple teachers speak of a restorative justice approach[6] as an important aspect of social justice. This means teachers help students deal with discipline issues through teaching, dialogue, and problem solving, as opposed to punishment. This reveals itself in the discussion about Lupe, and the restorative justice approach is repeatedly offered as the reason the school had only two suspensions during the 2011–12 academic year.

Students first. The community presses for decision making that puts the students' needs above all others when priorities, schedules, and budgets are set. Developing relationships with students is the first way to demonstrate this value. This aligns with efforts across the country to encourage greater connectedness among students, teachers, and curriculum (Darling-Hammond, Ross, & Milliken, 2007; Klem & Connell, 2004; Steinberg & Allen, 2002).

Leaders also put students first is by keeping the school small and allocating as many resources as possible to hiring teachers, to lower the teacher-student ratio. Small schools are more likely to create the right conditions for student connection, equity, and high achievement (Raywid, 1996; Sizer, 1984; Wasley et al., 2000).

Rigorous intellectual and personal development for everyone. High achievement that leads to students' college success is paramount, and here, the development of thoughtfulness, empathy, civic engagement, and leadership are just as important. Students learn about historical events while confronting the historical and current realities of power, race, class, and culture. At the same time, they are invited to ponder the betterment of themselves and their communities.

High achievement and continuous challenge and learning is an equal expectation of teachers. They are to be strong in their content area and pedagogy, eager in outreach to and support of students beyond the classroom, and reflective as practitioners and colleagues.

Democratic participation. The organization has "horizontal leadership," with different teachers taking responsibility for pieces of work historically assumed by a principal. And the principal has roles that are traditionally a teacher's, namely supporting student mentors. Decisions are made collaboratively among teachers, and students are engaged as participants in teacher feedback, in student advising, and hiring staff. This involvement extends to families and community partners.

PROFESSIONAL LEARNING FOCUSES ON EACH STUDENT AS A PERSON AND A LEARNER

Supporting Teachers to Understand and Engage Students as Persons

A range of practices illustrates how teachers personalize the school experience (see Figure 3.2). These speak to research demonstrating that the more students experience personalization, the greater their level of engagement and connection to school (Fredricks, Blumenfeld, & Paris, 2004) and even achievement (McClure, Yonezawa, & Jones, 2010).

The heart of personalizing is the Advisory Program. This supports research that asserts that the most effective practices appear to be small schools, advisory programs, and like-minded reforms intent on improving youth-adult relationships (Yonezawa, McClure, & Jones, 2012). The Advisory Curriculum is highly structured and designed to provide students skills in knowledge of self and community, improving study skills and organization, navigating college application and rigor, and character development. Advisory takes place for one hour daily, Monday through Thursday. Days have a specific focus: college preparation (Mondays), academic support and intervention (Tuesdays and Thursdays), and character education drawing on Facing History and Ourselves curriculum (Wednesdays). Each grade level has a particular emphasis. (See online resources for a detailed description of the Advisory framework.)

Professional learning time—and inevitably time beyond that—seeks to help teachers develop dispositions and skills that honor students as

Figure 3.2 School Practices That Show How Each Student Matters

- **Advisory for four hours weekly.** This curriculum has a different emphasis during each of the four years. (See description in online resources.)
- **Student-led conferences.** These 15- to 30-minute conferences take place in the evening twice yearly with all of the student's teachers and family members participating. Each teacher creates his or her own supporting materials.
- **Very Important Person (VIP) meetings.** These meetings are convened when multiple teachers have concerns regarding a student's academic performance or personal behavior. The student's teachers and family discuss what supports are needed in a particular situation, and how to collectively work on them.
- **Publicly posted, individual student academic progress every five weeks.** These name progress and areas of need. They are coded as gold and silver (both on track to qualify for University of California admission), bronze (on track to qualify for California State college admission), and red (student needs support).
- **Having peer mentors.** Students share experiences, ask for advice, share concerns about academic and personal experiences, and generally have another member of the community as a touch point and advocate.
- **Being peer mentors.** Selected 10th, 11th, and 12th grade students are trusted with looking at academic records of peers, sitting in on mentee IEP meetings as witnesses and advocates, flagging important community issues to faculty, and sharing experiences with fellow students.
- **Individual Pupil Education Plan.** This document will be used quarterly to more formally reflect on student's strengths and needs.
- **Teacher availability to confer before and after school**. It's not unusual for parents and students to have teacher phone numbers.
- **Twice-yearly student feedback to faculty on their teaching.** Surveys are administered to students, and a group of students compile the trends and present them to the faculty.
- **Participation in teacher hiring.** Students participate in interviews, debriefs, and decision-making conversations.

active community members (e.g., through being on hiring committees, giving colleagues feedback on teaching), and support conferencing with families and community resources. These school practices require teachers to hone skills in asking probing questions of students, understanding standards, and how to scaffold learning for each student; assess the motivations, learning styles, and academic strengths of each student; plan instruction; and give feedback that specifically points students and families to the next level of proficiency, as a next step toward college success. Grade teams are the go-to resource for this work. Some support may be through peer observations, some through asking for advice or getting oriented to protocols or curriculum materials. Friday afternoon professional development sessions, held in the Collaboration Room, dedicate some time to supporting the work in advisory and to curriculum development. Morning meetings allow for VIP meetings, in-the-moment situations that need attention, and grade team collaboration regarding students.

Mr. Navarro emphasizes that for teachers to be compassionate with students, they must also be compassionate with one another. He has weekly opportunities for all members of the community to engage in acts of kindness, and designs professional learning activities like the one described in Figure 3.3 that support educators grounding their professional work in respect for one another as persons.

Figure 3.3 Professional Learning Experience: A Leadership Metaphor

Homework Given Before a Staff Gathering

You are invited to reflect on your journey as a person, an educator, and a leader. Please bring in an object that is a metaphor for your road to leadership as an educator. Be prepared to talk about your experience.

On Site

The leader frames why this is important. Educators need to remember one another as persons.

Each teacher has five minutes to tell the story of their journey, and to describe their style of leadership.

The group reflects on their collective gifts, and what they provide for students and one another.

Purpose of the Tool: This exercise supports educators understanding each other as persons and as leaders, and their deepening respect and trust for one another.

Unique Use at SJ Humanitas: This exercise underscores that all teachers are leaders, and all educators have overcome and continue to have struggles, as students have. Teachers are asked to guide a similar activity with students at the beginning of the school year.

Reflection: In what ways does your professional development encourage you to know your colleague as persons, to understand what is most important to them about being an educator? How might "knowing the humanity" of other teachers help support equity in your school community?

Interdisciplinary Curriculum as a Way to Support Teachers to Engage Students as Persons

The Los Angeles Education Partnership (LAEP) is a critical partner beyond and within the classroom. Their Humanitas program (see boxed text) provides the framework and grounding professional learning for thematic curriculum. It is grounded by research (Aschbacher, 1991; Newmann & Wehlage, 1995; VanTassel-Baska et al., 2008), the California standards, and Wiggins and McTighe's (2005) "backwards mapping." Essential questions and enduring understandings frame lessons and units, and assessments exist in three forms: an extended writing assignment, a multiple-choice test developed in the style of the California Standards Test (CST) required for college applications, and a performance or demonstration. Humanitas professional development provides teachers the foundational knowledge and skills to form teams, identify interdisciplinary themes, unwrap the standards and develop unit and lesson plans, develop interdisciplinary writing assignments and rubrics they need, and score the rubrics.

Leading Partner: Los Angeles Education Partnership (LAEP)

LAEP brokers and provides services to support college awareness, college counseling, tutoring, youth leadership, and youth development

LAEP's Humanitas Small School Network has four elements:

1. An instructional model, in which teachers develop thematic, interdisciplinary units to engage their students

2. A network of teachers in LAUSD who collaborate and attend professional development to refine their craft

3. The identity of over 40 Small Learning Communities and small schools in LAUSD

4. A branch of Los Angeles Education Partnership (LAEP) that supports the work of these teachers

Source: from Humanitas website, retrieved July 5, 2012, from http://www.laep.org/humanitas/About.html.

To see a range of award-winning interdisciplinary units, go to: http://www.laep.org/humanitas/Lessons.html.

LAEP shapes a range of professional learning opportunities that sustain the community of Humanitas educators across Los Angeles.

The school has added its own strategies to the model to address individual learning needs, and leaders offer professional learning sessions to the Humanitas network. Each student (and teacher) completes a styles preference self-assessment based on Gardner's theory of multiple intelligences (2000; see online resources for websites related to multiple intelligences). The lesson-planning template includes space for teachers to name how they will engage at least four intelligences during the lesson. And because of the significant number of English Language Learners, teachers integrate second language learning strategies into lessons. Plus the school's special education teacher supports inclusion strategies within the interdisciplinary model across the school. The interdisciplinary work has started with a focus on integrating English, history, and art, and is extending into every subject, first by supporting teachers to use similar teaching strategies, and then by weaving content into the unit themes.

To support continuous creativity, moral and civic thinking, and general rigor of content, the school works very closely with Facing History and Ourselves (see boxed text). Faculty members

Leading Partner: Facing History and Ourselves

We work with educators throughout their careers to improve their effectiveness in the classroom, as well as their students' academic performance and civic learning. Through a rigorous investigation of the events that led to the Holocaust, as well as other recent examples of genocide and mass violence, students in a Facing History class learn to combat prejudice with compassion, indifference with participation, and myth and misinformation with knowledge.

Source: from the Facing History and Ourselves website: http://www.facing.org/aboutus

Professional Development

Our programs serve educators who understand that their students' academic and emotional growth depends to a large degree on their own commitment to growing and learning. We work with middle and high school teachers, helping them to master important skills in classroom pedagogy: how to conduct a discussion in which students truly talk and listen to one another; how to raise controversial topics; how to establish a classroom atmosphere of trust.

Source: from http://www2.facinghistory.org/campus/events.nsf/professionaldevelopment?readform

For a range of lesson plans, videos, and other resources, go to: http://www.facing.org/educator-resources-0

identify topics they want to explore, and sessions on those topics are presented monthly. During the 2011–12 school year, Social Justice Humanitas teachers had a personal exploration of issues such as the U.S. timing for getting involved in World War II and what that means for our national responsibility regarding the Holocaust. Teachers discern this individually and as a group, in order to understand these concepts in depth and be able to apply them across the grade level and across the content areas. Teachers' collective knowledge provides an entry point for students to make personal meaning of those historical moments and connect them to their own contexts and lives. At SJ Humanitas, this kind of teacher learning is not a one-time event, but occurs continuously as units are developed and defined. Teachers will learn the content that those in other disciplines teach, in order to weave key concepts into their own lessons.

Facing History's body of research shows that their approach

- increases teachers' capacity to effectively create student and community-centered learning environments;
- increases teachers' ability to broaden students' historical understanding and social and civic responsibility; and
- increases educators' professional engagement, satisfaction, and sense of personal accomplishment.

With the building blocks for this work from Humanitas, and continuous prompts to enrich content from Facing History, it falls to teachers to adapt, apply, and integrate their learning into relevant, engaging, and rigorous units of study. This happens primarily on the grade-level team, and then with colleagues of similar subjects or others who may help with specific topics. The dynamic of ongoing adult dialogue and collaboration interweaves with questions students bring, insights they have, and lack of understanding they have. All these together press teachers to dig deeper to ask the right questions, or reframe a particular interdisciplinary prompt or assignments. When teachers of multiple disciplines do this work together, they are supporting each other in increasing rigor and naturally embedding peer review, as Mr. Navarro noted.

Supporting Both Student and Teacher
Understanding of Strengths and Needs

To build on the work of interdisciplinary teams advisory, teachers are thinking about how to ensure that information about student learning is tracked over time, and that there is dialogue and documentation about every student with regularity. As a result, Mr. Navarro and the special education teacher developed the Individual Plan, as shown in Figure 3.4.

The school leaders have a plan for discussing each student systematically as a team every five weeks and capturing key points of that conversation through the Individual Pupil Education Plan (IPEP). While even more budget cuts and related furlough days have cut time to do this systematically, the school will begin the practice by completing the forms and starting the review cycle for the students with the greatest struggles and the greatest academic strengths. This document also prompts teacher and student dialogue, formalizes teacher discussions about students, and keeps everyone honest about follow-through.

Time at the end and beginning of the school year complements the range of professional learning time during the school year. The three days of the August retreat, complete with overnight accommodations, are designed for the faculty to step away from the nitty-gritty. This is the time when colleagues contextualize the work that has been done, take stock of the big picture, and plan for instruction and professional learning.

> **Reflection:** What systems does your school have in place to track **and discuss** student progress regularly and over time? How do teachers come together to look at and document progress for each student so that each student receives the right level of support throughout the academic year?

The design of professional learning overall is the charge of the lead teachers, with many giving input. Table 3.3 illustrates a range of structures for professional learning.

LEADERSHIP AND SYSTEMS SUSTAIN EDUCATOR LEARNING

Expectations clear across a range of documents and practices. SJ Humanitas has a lot more documentation about their values and expectations than most schools. This is the fruit of intentionally building a philosophy and curriculum over 10 years. With each hire and expansion of a subject or a grade, the teachers intentionally sought to reinforce values of high expectations, personalization, democratic organization, and

Figure 3.4 Individual Pupil Education Plan

Student Name:	Teacher:	Date:

Present Level of Performance: **Grade: 9**

Mathematics **Course:** **Grade: A** ☐ **B** ☐ **C** ☐ **D** ☐ **F** ☐

Strengths: Please describe academic strengths.

Areas of Need: What are some areas that the student needs improvement on?

Organization: E ☐ S ☐ U ☐ **Work Habits:** E ☐ S ☐ U ☐

Cooperation: E ☐ S ☐ U ☐

	Negative	Average	Positive	N/A
Attitude toward school:	☐	☐	☐	☐
Attitude toward peers:	☐	☐	☐	☐
Attitude toward you:	☐	☐	☐	☐

Overall Concerns	**Solutions/Recommendations**
Type here	Type here

Other Comments:
Other information not covered above

Purpose of the Tool:
The Individual Pupil Education Plan (IPEP) can capture and summarize student strengths and needs in a narrative, and can travel with a student across time.

Unique Use at SJ Humanitas: This document catalyzes a conversation of teachers across subjects regarding individual students, and tracks feedback for the student, family, and future teachers.

Every five weeks, teachers analyze student attendance, behavior incidents, tardies, grades, and benchmark assessment scores.

Source: Social Justice Humanitas School. Used with permission.

Table 3.3 Individual, Team, and Whole School Learning at SJ Humanitas Academy

Individual Learning	Team Learning
Coaching and Modeling	*Grade-Level Teams*
A culture of classroom visits exists within and beyond grade-level teams. These quick visits to colleagues' classrooms provide an informal opportunity for teachers to model lessons and dialogue about curriculum and instruction.	Teams create thematic, interdisciplinary units, jointly assess student work and analyze the data, and determine intervention strategies.
Peer Observations	In the interdisciplinary model, team time is often focused on deepening teacher understanding of learning goals across content areas, and on ensuring multiple ways to explore important concepts. grade-level teams received a $500 stipend to meet over winter break to create curriculum units.
Teachers do peer observations using a protocol that is designed to offer peer feedback on practice. Observations are meant to be done quarterly; in the first year of implementation, teachers did this once.	
	Team Leadership
Self-Initiated Learning	Team leaders attend weekly leadership meetings, where team progress is reviewed and needs/next steps for teamwork are identified.
Teachers are expected to have deep subject matter in their field, and, more specifically, within their units of study. Teachers cultivate individual interests as they relate to deepening subject-matter expertise, knowledge of primary source materials, and pedagogy.	*Scheduled Team Time*
	Teachers have 30 minutes daily to touch base, address specific student needs, and address common issues for the day. Teams are scheduled to meet 100 minutes in each six-day cycle.

Whole School Learning

- Professional learning develops skills and dispositions that honor students as active community members (effectively running advisory, understanding varied learning styles of students, working with students' families)
- External partners frame key ideas with whole faculty; application of new learning happens within interdisciplinary teams.
- Annual summer and end-of-term reflections provide whole faculty analysis of progress, and big-picture planning, and team building.
- Weekly, two-hour meetings take place each Friday to focus on instruction, implementation of advisory curriculum, and to work with external partners.

social justice. The community's clarity was honed by having to advocate for resources, and then making the case to become a free-standing, public pilot school. This distinct evolution required extensive thinking and

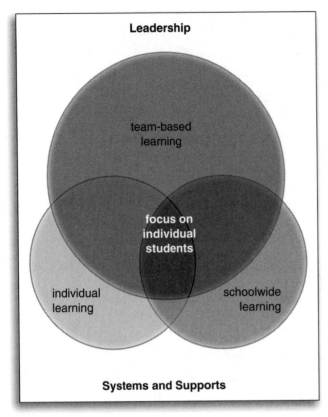

writing about identity, specific plans and practices, and accomplishments.

To hire the right staff, the job descriptions and interview processes seek to be very clear about emphasizing Students First and teacher collaboration. Because SJ Humanitas is a pilot school, teachers sign an Elect-to-Work Agreement that delineates the specifics of these commitments (see Figure 3.5).

Professional learning is grounded in understanding student needs, looking at their levels of success, and figuring out what to do for students when they are and are not successful. These expectations translate into a set of guiding questions that consider why students are successful, how educators respond when they are and are not, and how they know their practice is successful. The boxed text clarifies how school leaders categorize expectations for professional learning by naming four categories for continuous adult learning.

Reflection, feedback, and more feedback. The interdisciplinary teaching model builds in a cycle of constant feedback and accountability on the level of rigor, the pacing of instruction, and how the instruction can improve in order to boost student learning. Beyond this foundation of feedback, which the community assumes will be used for reflection and improving practice, the leaders look to create additional feedback loops across the school. One is teacher peer feedback on practice (see Figure 3.6). Another is twice-yearly student feedback on their learning experiences.

National board for certified teachers (NBCTs). Another system to guarantee self-reflection is ensured by teachers' written commitment to become National Board Certified Teachers (NBCTs) within five years of joining the faculty. Three Design Team members are NBCTs, so they have gone through a process of preparing a portfolio of practice, sharing video of their practice and samples of student work, using a rubric to reflect on practice, and presenting the portfolio to colleagues. Leaders consider this range of reflective practices essential in a school committed to this level of collaborative practice (Berg, 2003).

Teacher feedback. Peer observation is grounded in the belief that teachers will want to learn from their colleagues' practice, that dialogue regarding practice is important for teacher growth, and that improved practice can result from this dialogue, just as peer conferencing/mentoring

Types of Professional Learning Expected at SJ Humanitas

- Foundation building. This includes frameworks and values regarding social justice, restorative justice, habits of mind, Understanding by Design, and Facing History and Ourselves.
- Capacity building. This includes team building, resiliency work, and plans for cognitive coaching and developing effective protocols for teaming and collaborative leadership.
- Curriculum and assessment. This includes interdisciplinary lesson planning, differentiated learning, strategies for English Language Learners, use of interactive notebooks, and culturally relevant and responsive pedagogy.
- Data analysis. This is emphasized in five-week data cycles where teams jointly analyze attendance and tardiness, behavior incidents, academic grades across the curriculum, and five-week benchmark assessments, which are administered the week prior to the full-faculty school-level review, which take place on scheduled Data Days.

Figure 3.5 Excerpt From SJ Humanitas Academy 2011–2012 Elect-to-Work Agreement

As a faculty member of Social Justice Humanitas Academy (SJHA), I understand I am asked to put students' needs first at all times. When planning the curriculum, I agree to work creatively to meet the diverse learning styles and needs of our student population. I have read and agree with the SJHA mission statement and intend to use project-based, constructive learning whenever possible in my curriculum. In order to do this, I agree to teach, plan, and reflect collaboratively. My lessons and curriculum will be developed by my teaching team, which will include my grade-level team teachers as well as other content specific teachers. I know that SJHA aims to have interdisciplinary curriculum therefore I will collaborate in horizontal, grade-level teams to develop standards-based interdisciplinary and integrated curriculum. I will also collaborate in vertical, subject-alike teams to create a coherent approach to skill building. In order to plan and implement this kind of curriculum I agree to meet with my teaching teams in order to assess students' needs, reflect on student work, and revise and develop curriculum.

Source: Social Justice Humanitas Academy Elect-to-Work Agreement, 2011–2012. Used with permission.

Note: For the full agreement, see online resources.

among students can result in growth. One focus is on supporting the learning of the observing teacher who wants to understand a particular colleague's practice, and dialogue related to the work. The Peer Observation Action Plan document (see Figure 3.6) seeks to lift up effective practice, "Teacher Genius" as Mr. Navarro calls it, so that the work can be further shared in the future. Teachers identify practices that they would like to observe, and all teachers are asked to observe peers four times during the year. In this first year as a free-standing pilot school, they accomplished one observation cycle per teacher, more if schedules allowed for observation without a substitute. If a peer observation reveals substandard performance, the template also has space for the observing teacher to recommend very specific supports. Any observing teacher can offer these. All teachers are encouraged to reach out to one another, if they see a colleague struggling with their craft. This is easier for some than others, particularly as new teachers come to the school and the system encounters scheduling challenges, since the observing and observed teacher schedules need to match up; otherwise classroom coverage is needed. In all cases, the protocol includes a Post-Observation Reflection (see Figure 3.7), so that the observed teacher can document his or her comments on the observation and supporting written Action Plan. Beyond this formal

Figure 3.6   Peer Observation Action Plan

Strengths

Identify strengths.
Spread the wealth: How might the teacher share these strengths with the team?

Support

Identify areas of need.
Explain support plan. This could include observations of other teachers, professional development, structured mentoring, etc.

Follow-up

How and when will the observer follow up with the observed teacher?

Purpose of the Tool: The observing teacher(s) draft a document with observations.

Unique Use at SJ Humanitas: Teachers and leaders use this form to encourage an ongoing dialogue on practice, both through lifting up specific practices to be shared with other teachers, and through calling for a time when the observed and observing teachers will reconvene.

Source: Social Justice Humanitas Academy Leadership Team. Used with permission.

process, multiple teachers spoke of their "culture of observation," as they will stop in one another's classroom for short periods of time simply to learn about a particular practice, or to understand how a colleague is teaching a particular lesson.

> **Reflection:** What formal and informal mechanisms for peer observation exist at your school? Is there a peer-observation culture at your school, and does it promote peer dialogue about what a teacher can do to improve? If not, what might need to happen at your school to support a model where teachers provide direct feedback to each other about improving practice?

Student feedback. Students complete surveys regarding each teacher and advisor twice yearly (see Figure 3.8). These supplement district-required evaluations, with a Pass/Fail framework. But these do not rise to the level of substantive feedback that school leaders believe can support continuous instructional improvement.

Their surveys complement discussions about the learning experience that students have, in service of understanding and integrating the student perspective into teacher planning. The following passage, from the Humanitas Pilot School Proposal describes the student feedback process:

> Student input regarding curriculum and culture is also invited through a series of steering committee meetings that occur at least once a semester. Students choose representatives from each grade level. These representatives poll their peers regarding their educational experience, both pro and con. Armed with this feedback, student representatives meet with teachers in grade level teams and respond to teacher-posed questions, as well as giving unsolicited feedback based on the input from their peers. The student perspective is very important to the design of the professional development agenda at the Humanitas Academy (p. 34).

The student feedback process is not easily embraced by every teacher, but the Design Team upholds the importance of this data point to inform school improvements and professional learning specifically.

Figure 3.7 Post-Observation Reflection

Create context.
Create context and provide background information that is necessary to understand the lesson or any behaviors/incidents that the observer may have observed or noted.
Respond to observations.
Which details noted in your observation stood out to you? Why?

Purpose of the Tool: This document is designed to ensure the observed teacher's response to the proposed Teacher Action Plan, and to support reflection on the observations.

Source: Social Justice Humanitas Academy Leadership Team. Used with permission.

Inching their way to a Japanese model: professional learning as sustainable. This community does not dodge the challenging students or the hard issues within their community. While they continue to settle into their new building and reach far, they are also honest about how they need to improve their professional community. The leaders at the school understand they have a time-intensive interdisciplinary model that demands everyone's collaboration and that is intensified further by evolving from a small learning community to a pilot high school in a new building. In their accreditation report, the leaders name the need for more organized, focused, and efficient meetings, and communications systems that better facilitate collaborative support of individual students and collaborative decision making. And they understand that they are pushing on the boundaries of the teaching profession and current organization of schools by shaping a high school with extremely high expectations and results, while having the school also be teacher led. This combination of aspirations pushes on existing structures in Los Angeles, as it would virtually in any community in the country.

The reality of welcoming a large group of new teachers into the school culture and practices further forces the point. The original teachers who evolved the model carefully recognize the number of practices, values, expectations, and collective habits of mind that need to be made explicit and to be taught to new colleagues, at the same time that they seek to be open to new learnings and possibilities. This can be a challenge both for the practiced teachers, as they seek a high level and consistency of practice in realizing their design, as it is for teachers coming new to the school, who may not have understood exactly how much it takes for an urban high school to enjoy so much student success.

Figure 3.8 SJ Humanitas Academy Student Survey

A = Strongly Agree; B = Agree; C = Disagree; D = Strongly Disagree; E = N/A

Content Area Teacher

1. My teachers use DPAs/Planners effectively in order to keep track of my assignments.
2. I believe the use of DPAs/Planners is helping me become a more successful student.
3. My teachers provide enough after-school tutoring to support my learning.
4. The interdisciplinary lessons taught by my teachers are effective in connecting the material to other classes.
5. My advisory class provides the structure and opportunity to support my academic needs.
6. I feel supported by my peers and mentors.
7. I feel safe and accepted in the Humanitas Academy.
8. Teachers in the Humanitas Academy have high expectations.
9. I am treated fairly and with respect by my Humanitas teachers.
10. I would recommend the Humanitas Academy to other students.

Advisory Teacher

81. My advisory teacher provides a safe and respectful environment in my class.
82. My advisory teacher provides the class with meaningful and actionable information on college—i.e., applications, finances, degrees, etc.
83. My advisory teacher is well prepared and delivers effective lessons.
84. My advisory teacher supports students emotionally and academically.
85. My advisory teacher consistently monitors student progress by checking Grades, DPAs, and Student Planners.

Purpose of the Tool:
(As written in the slide presentation shared with students):

- Gather information and insight from students.
- Ensure that the needs of our students are being met.
- Identify where to focus resources.
- Make better, more informed decisions.
- Identify the need for change.

Unique Purpose of the Tool at SJ Humanitas: These 10 questions are posed to students regarding each of their teachers, and their advisory teacher, twice yearly.

A group of students have a conversation with peers following the collection of this data, and ask about general experiences of teaching instruction and teachers. Those students capture these comments, and share them, along with their own, with teachers.

Source: Samantha Siegeler and José Navarro. (2012). Social Justice Humanitas Academy Leadership Team. Used with permission.

NOTES

1.   School demographics citation: Social Justice Humanitas Academy State Exam Test Results: http://star.cde.ca.gov/star2012/ViewReport.aspx?ps=true&lst TestYear=2012&lstTestType=C&lstCounty=19&lstDistrict=64733–000&lst School=0124388&lstGroup=1&lstSubGroup=1

2.   Pilot schools are a concept developed as part of the Boston Public Schools/ Boston Teachers Union contract in the early 1994. For more on Los Angeles pilot schools, go to: http://www.utla.net/pilot. Retrieved September 21, 2012.

3.   Communication with Samantha Siegeler, lead teacher, September 23, 2012.

4.   Students' names are changed. Educators' actual names are in the text.

5.   See Banks (2004), and Sleeter and Grant (2006). Multicultural education must attend to all students (not just the ones from traditionally marginalized groups) and represent the perspectives of a range of peoples and backgrounds, including those represented within the school community. Effective practice advances antiracism and supports understanding one's personal stance and perspective, and respectfully engaging those with different perspectives.

6.   See Yang (2009) and www.restorativejustice.org. Restorative justice emphasizes repairing the harm caused or revealed by criminal behavior. It involves cooperative processes that seek to repair harm, and seeks to transform traditional relationships within communities.

The Variables Are Time and Support   **4**

Montgomery Center School (PreK–8),
Montgomery Center, Vermont

> *"You're a 1. I'm going to get you to a 2. By the time you leave fifth grade, you're going to be a 3 in math. You believe me. You will be. And I'm going to throw you a party."*
> *"You'll throw me a party?"*
> *"You go from a 1 to a 3—I'll throw you a party!"*
> *And so we're doing practice tests. And I correct him.*
> *"You didn't read the directions, did you?"*
> *"No," he says.*
> *He was distracted. He did one part out of the three. It was so simple a change.*
> *"[If you read the directions] That right there will pull you up to a 2 or a 3. Then with the Vmath..."*
>
> *—Jeffrey Ward, Montgomery Center School math teacher,*
> *describing a conversation with a fifth-grade math student*

That's a typical exchange at Montgomery Center School (Montgomery), either during class or perhaps at lunchtime, when teachers often eat with the students. Beth O'Brien has been cultivating learning and collaboration there for 23 years, first as teacher, then teaching principal, now principal. The preK–8 school has 155 students in a town with a population of 1,201 (U.S. Census Bureau, 2010). The parents of children at the school work seasonally in construction or the nearby Jay Peak Ski Resort, or as teachers, food servers, home-based telecommuters, or people working with border patrol (Picus, Odden, Glenn, Griffith, & Wolkoff, 2012). Over the years, the student population has held steady, while the percentage of special education students has decreased. Mrs. O'Brien attributes this to changes in instruction and support.

Montgomery Center School

Demographics and Commendations

Grades Taught: PreK through 8

Number of Students: 127

Percentage Eligible for Free and Reduced-Price Lunch: 54%

Special Education: 11%

Racial/Ethnic Percentages:

- Hispanic: 0%
- Black: 1%
- White: 97%
- Asian/Pacific Island: 0%
- Other: 2% (multiracial)

Sampling of School/Educator Achievements:

- 2011—School recognized by Vermont Department of Education for best effort throughout the state in narrowing the achievement gap consistently over several years, as it tracked a cohort of students over time. The Department noted little difference between performance of those eligible and not eligible for free and reduced-price lunch.
- National Distinguished Principal of Vermont, 2012

SMALL AND MIGHTY

The school has outperformed the district and the state, and is being asked to share their approach to improving achievement. When leaders from the school do talk about their success, they are quick to speak to student outcomes being a starting point, specifically, their goal for every student to score at least 80% on every test or equivalent, indicating proficiency. Results of the New England Common Assessment (NECAP) have improved consistently since 2004 (see Figure 4.1).

JOURNEY

Mrs. O'Brien is clear about this not being an overnight success. "This is not about having some great teachers. It's about every student and every teacher working hard over a long time." Jeffrey Ward, a 35-year veteran at the school, understands this well. Originally he taught middle-grade reading and social studies. Now he teaches fourth- and fifth-grade math and eighth-grade social studies, plus physical education in grades 5 through 8. He speaks of the days in the old building, before 1990, "No one ever came in [your classroom]. You were on your own. You needed help? You'd better find it." Teachers on the first floor did not talk to those on the second. "Then Beth came. She came upstairs to talk with people."

When Mrs. O'Brien became principal in 1999, she knew she had to cultivate an environment for everyone learning. "If you want people to grow individually, you've got to make them comfortable taking a risk." She

Figure 4.1 Montgomery Center School State Assessment Scores 2006–2011

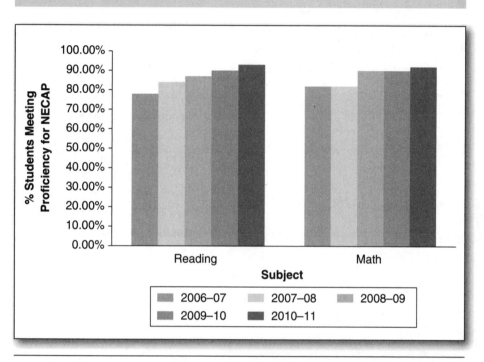

Source: Vermont Department of Education, http://edw.vermont.gov/ReportServer/Pages/ ReportViewer.aspx?%2fPublic%2fNECAP+Assessment+Report (retrieved on December 1, 2012).

first worked on "decorum": developing a safe and respectful learning environment where everyone can contribute. To build that understanding and culture, Mrs. O'Brien combined resources for the character education program over time: Responsive Classroom, FISH philosophy, among others. Mrs. O'Brien was clear at the beginning that a different culture and way of being together was essential. "It's not about great teachers or good teachers working in isolation. If we want to effect change, we have to have a systemic approach."

Crystal Johnson interviewed at Montgomery 13 years ago, two days before her wedding. She was hired as a grade 3–4 multiage teacher, and became literacy coach under a Reading First grant. For the last five years she has taught first grade. She says the faculty started talking about their practice in Critical Friends groups in 2002. "I was new. I did not trust people . . . not because they gave me a reason not to. I didn't know how to talk about what I do. That was your *secret.*"

What does Mr. Ward remember as a major shift at the school? The charge given to the faculty once Critical Friends were underway, and they

Thinkers and Texts That Influence Montgomery

- Richard DuFour, Robert Eaker, and Rebecca DuFour (Eds.), *On Common Ground: The Power of Professional Learning Communities* (2005)
- Richard DuFour, Rebecca DuFour, Robert Eaker, and Thomas Many, *Learning by Doing: A Handbook for Professional Learning Communities at Work* (2006)
- Robert Marzano, *The Art and Science of Teaching: A Comprehensive Framework for Effective Instruction* (2007)
- Doug Reeves, *The Learning Leader: How to Focus School Improvement for Better Results* (2006)
- Mike Schmoker, *Focus: Elevating the Essentials to Radically Improve Student Learning* (2011)

started professional learning communities (PLCs):

> I think one of the biggest things for me is when Beth said to me, "We've got to make sure the kids understand what our goals are. I said, "What are you talking about?" She goes, "Like 80%. Now our kids know that we want 80% [mastery on all their assignments]." I said, "It can't make that big of a difference to tell a kid that. They want to do well anyway." I was shocked . . . it's crazy. And I'll still question it. Because I say, "80% is good. Now we want 83%, 85%, 87%. It's got to stop somewhere. Kids can only be pushed so hard, and we can only push so hard." But they keep meeting the challenge.

Mrs. Johnson remembers some anxiety around teams setting goals as well. "I remember my group being nervous about SMART goals, not knowing if your kids would meet them. And were we going to be evaluated on that. . . . Now we set goals as high as 100%" of student mastery of essential skills and knowledge.

The teachers are clear that it's their fundamental work to figure out what students need, and to provide the right help at the right time. The expectations are immutable. "Several years ago we had a shift from a focus on teaching to a focus on student learning. You do this with a focus on assessment. The variables in improving learning become time and support for learning," explains Mrs. O'Brien. Kristina Bowen, preK and kindergarten teacher pulls out samples of student work as she explains how she helped one kindergartener:

> One of my lower students . . . came to me, and he hated writing. He has very week finger muscles, so he has a sponge and all these

different things [to help with muscle development]. He started school later in the year [than the other students], and the thought of writing a story overwhelmed him. He could not come up with a story, and I knew we had been practicing [as a class] for a long time. So what I did with him was first I started writing in yellow and he had to trace over it. And I said, "You know what, this doesn't make sense to me because he's not writing. He's just tracing. What a waste of time."

Mrs. Bowen pondered the situation and shifted strategies. She had him "cut out pictures that he liked and I said, 'Write a sentence to match that.' He loved it, because he had pictures that he picked, and he started writing. So I thought that was great for him. He liked it. He took more ownership . . . 'And I can show Mom.' He did this on his own."

MULTIGRADE PROFESSIONAL LEARNING COMMUNITIES (PLCS) WITH KIDS AT THE CENTER

Sometimes teacher puzzle out solutions on their own; often they turn to their PLC. Figuring out how to make teachers comfortable with PLCs in a school with 10 full-time teachers, and several part-time teachers and staff, initially took some doing. Organizing them while having only one teacher for each grade "was a huge challenge when I first got here," shares Mrs. O'Brien. She attended multiple conferences with the DuFours: "The philosophy made sense to me. We could not work harder so we needed to do things differently if we wanted to get better results." Since 2006, there are three multigrade PLCs: grades 6–8, grades 3–5 and preK–2 or 3. "Grade 3 was a question. Sometimes the third grade works with K, 1, 2, and sometimes they work with 4, 5," depending on the agenda." The primary and first, second, and third grades have teachers who all teach the same content to students. The middle grade teachers teach different content, but teach the same students. Grades 4 and 5 are partially departmentalized.

Today, PLCs are understood as the forum and framework for how student outcomes are named, measured, and planned out. Steve Moran, middle school math teacher who came to Montgomery five years ago, talks about the middle school PLC. "We meet often. What I find different [at this school] is the amount we get done—the task or focus of the team. That's Sara. Sara is our team leader. She is very organized. We are all on board. We have our norms, and we have the vision."

The middle-grade PLC members talk about how they spend their time:

Ms. Zeineth-Collins	A lot of the time we spend talking about certain kids and what's happening in our classrooms, kind of comparing notes with each other saying, "Is the child having the same problems in your class? If not, what are you doing?" So that we're . . . feeding off of each other in that way. We also spend a lot of time going over data; going over the different kinds of assignments that we're doing. If the kids aren't getting it, either we tweak it, or [consider] what kinds of interventions do we put in for that kid. Or if there's a group of kids who are not getting it, how do we intervene there in a bigger way to cover more kids? And as we see that a kid needs more help we go up the pyramid until we're totally on that one kid to help him out.
Interviewer	As you think about groups of kids, is it more looking at who's not making the mark, and focusing your energies on talking about them?
Ms. Zeineth-Collins	That's the way we've done that in the past. . . . [Now] it's more, "Who's the next group that with the smallest amount of interventions will succeed?" . . . Then focus on the group that needs more time. So we're making sure that we're getting them [all the students] up there at the same time, so that they [all] are functioning at the proficiency level.
Interviewer	Going with the easy kids first helps you with the AYP [Annual Yearly Progress], right?
Ms. Zeineth-Collins	AYP is wonderful, but it's not AYP. It's about the kids, so we need to keep that in mind.
Mr. Moran	I don't think I ever looked at it as AYP, it's just where the kids are.
Ms. Caldwell	I think of it as our SMART goals. We have very specific goals, and in terms of who's where in achieving the SMART goal, and what it would take [to move them ahead]. Like Sue [Ms. Zeineth-Collins] said, with the easier ones all we need to do is tweak it this way; paying attention to the different groupings, and what interventions would be necessary. But I never think of AYP either.

Ms. Zeineth-Collins	The other part is when we have reteach. . . . These are the kids who need the extra help, who are just about there. You give instructions to a para-educator in the room to work with those kids. And [then] you have time to work with those kids or the ones who are on level . . . that's how we organize our reteach.
Mr. Moran	More qualified teachers should be with the more needy students.

The PLC process, including tracking progress with daily assessments, shifts the desired outcome from teaching a class to student results. This requires deep understanding of the standards, instruction, and additional interventions. The school has evolved different supports—extra teacher help, Homework Club, tutoring, and reteach. In the reteach model, teachers spend concentrated time each day devoted to supporting students who have not met the benchmark for performance on current work, and extending the learning of students who have.

Students know that teachers are taking time for them outside the classroom and in. In a group interview, middle students (not their real names) reveal that they definitely know the goals, and that both teachers and students have essential roles:

Sara	They don't [baby you], and they have expectations; they expect you to get your work done.
Alexa	You can't get out of it easily.
Sara	You have to be responsible—responsibility or fail.

Students talk about the range of ways to improve when someone needs extra help. They name the list of reteach strategies and extra help by heart. If someone needs help, "It's not that they're not good at it. It's just that they need a little more understanding."

Ongoing reflection and feedback. It's assumed here that everyone has issues requiring a little more understanding once in a while, and that everyone has areas of expertise. A range of practices ensures that dialogue about teaching and learning goes beyond PLCs. Mrs. O'Brien tries to visit every classroom every day to see what's happening and check on needs. She writes notes to teachers reflecting what she saw, and increasingly sends feedback electronically. The teachers do walk-throughs as well, at least twice yearly, sometimes with Mrs. O'Brien and sometimes without. They are looking for specific colleague practices they can emulate or adapt. If a practice is not up to snuff, or there is resistance to collaboration, that's the principal's job. One teacher responds, "Beth would have discussed it with them by now. They wouldn't stay."

Continuing to raise the bar: Common Core. Improvement here is not an activity, it is a way of being. Mrs. O'Brien did not wait for the state or district to announce the guidelines for professional learning. She knew the Common Core was in the air: going deeper with content.

The Common Core is in evidence in the first-grade classroom, where a group of teachers are sitting at a students' table as they start their weekly professional learning community (PLC) meeting. They are doing a joint self-assessment of their primary PLC, the same self-assessment they completed in September. They are naming things they need to fix or try. Conversations reference work on the Common Core, how they introduced Common Core content that seemed too challenging, while some students rose to it. They talk about how this is changing their curriculum maps, and what's on next year's horizon. The conversation is not willy-nilly. One teacher sums it up this way: "It's very purposeful—Beth as a leader. She has one whole vision."

ANALYSIS

On the surface, Montgomery's success may seem straightforwardly like strong instructional leadership and a willing group of teachers attending to sensible recommendations, yet the particulars of their journey provide a roadmap. When Mrs. O'Brien became teaching principal there were big culture shifts that needed to take place—and no shortcuts. The work required attention to values practices that could permeate the entire system, ensuring appropriate attention to each student. A range of protocols and routines, and intentional innovations that evolved over time, have created a community that is collectively focused on and attentive to assessment, and continually recalibrating the support and time needed for each student to do well.

SCHOOL VALUES MADE EXPLICIT AND VISIBLE

Ensure every student achieves proficiency on every test. While benchmarks are set for writing using rubrics, and different subjects at different grades signaling proficiency, this is the general rule of thumb. Implicit in this idea is the assumption that every student can be proficient—and will be. This is public and unquestioned among teachers, students, families, and the community.

Stick with it until you get it right, together. Students are clear that they have to work hard, and that teachers will help them meet learning goals. Teachers stick with their goals for proficiency in math, writing, and reading until students attain mastery, whether it requires reteach strategies, extra time on task for students, or another sort of intervention. Every effort is made to help every student and teacher succeed. There is collaboration between students and teachers, and among teachers.

Improve continually. Everyone talks about how to best help students. They collect data, observe, maybe get some advice from colleagues, and make their best assessment of what's needed in each situation. If it does not work, they assess why, and test another hypothesis. When they get it right, they move on to the next issue, building on and sharing what they learned.

Think globally, act locally. National reform movements and their motives are important and respected, and when adopted, reforms are adopted thoroughly and universally. But the local educators and their needs and context are equally valued, and adaptation of reforms is key for them to take hold.

Trust teacher skill and professionalism. Mrs. O'Brien spoke of the concept of "loose-tight management," where the expectation and the schoolwide approaches are made clear, but individual teachers are responsible for figuring out how to adapt them in their own classrooms. This respect for teachers to know their students and apply professional judgment was evident in the discussions of achievement, climate, and assessment.

PROFESSIONAL LEARNING FOCUSES ON EACH STUDENT AS A PERSON AND A LEARNER

Supporting independent and professional thinking and problem solving regarding individual students. Mrs. O'Brien translates tight-loose management by selecting the best reforms she can find, introducing them to staff, taking time for understanding and buy-in, and then allowing teachers to adapt the practice to their own style. In turn, teachers are charged to try out a range of practices that exist within the agreed-upon frameworks and programs, and see what works for the students. Teachers have flexibility to assess a student's abilities and needs, and then based on the data and their knowledge of the students, they try out different practices that they think could work. This was illustrated in the earlier example of Kristina Bowen supporting a pre-schooler's prewriting skills development. Team meetings provide a space for discussions of how to support individual students, on what to try next. There's not a need to get it right the first time, but the imperative to work until it is right for each student.

From Critical Friends to professional learning communities. Not every Critical Friends Group (CFG) or professional learning community (PLC) across the country intends or claims to lead to personalization. But at Montgomery, these two constructs are used to understand each student as a learner, and then to figure out how to support him or her.

Critical Friends Groups (CFG). Developed by Annenberg Institute for School Reform, Critical Friends Groups was adopted by Montgomery in 2002 to launch significant schoolwide improvement and collaboration (see Figure 4.2 for CFG description). Before that, while many teachers were working independently with their students, they did not have consistently high-reaching goals.

CFGs provide norms, guidelines, and scaffolds designed to ensure a safe environment for bringing up challenging issues that can otherwise make teachers feel vulnerable. Specific protocols are matched to the desired outcome for the dialogue. At Montgomery, teachers in pairs had two-hour sessions monthly, based on the instructional or achievement issue they wanted to discuss and resolve. As teachers became comfortable with the protocols and as trust between and among teachers increased, the CFG became a vehicle for addressing vertical curriculum alignment and achievement gap issues. CFGs taught Montgomery teachers how to be safe in dialogue with one another. The model values and teaches equal participation of members, as well as getting to instructional substance. Teachers call upon these protocols to reinforce practices and ensure that there is a clear and supportive framework for conversations. They have used the model over time, and continue to use the protocols in after-school professional development sessions, including some of the work dedicated to the Common Core.

Critical Friends Protocols in Use at Montgomery School

Protocols are guidelines and steps for engaging in purposeful dialogue. The National School Reform Faculty has catalogued a range of protocols for different adult learning scenarios. Two favorites at Montgomery are:

1. Block Party

2. Save the Last Word for Me

To view these protocols, and find the full range of available protocols, see online resources.

Figure 4.2　Descriptions of Critical Friends Groups (CFGs) and Professional Learning Communities (PLCs)

What is a Critical Friends Group (CFG)?

A CFG is a learning community consisting of approximately 8–12 educators who come together voluntarily at least once a month for about two hours. Group members are committed to improving their practice through collaborative learning.

What are the purposes of a Critical Friends Group?

Critical Friends Groups are designed to:

- Create a professional learning community
- Make teaching practice explicit and public by "talking about teaching"
- Help people involved in schools to work collaboratively in democratic, reflective communities (Bambino, 2002)
- Establish a foundation for sustained professional development based on a spirit of inquiry (Dana, Silva, & Snow-Gerono, 2002)
- Provide a context to understand our work with students, our relationships with peers, and our thoughts, assumptions, and beliefs about teaching and learning
- Help educators help each other turn theories into practice and standards into actual student learning
- Improve teaching and learning

What are the characteristics of a professional learning community?

Professional learning communities are strong when teachers demonstrate:

- Shared norms and values
- Collaboration
- Reflective dialogue
- Deprivatization of practice
- Collective focus on student learning
- Spirit of shared responsibility for the learning of all students

Professional learning communities can develop when there is:

- Time to meet and talk
- Physical proximity
- Interdependent teaching roles
- Active communication structures
- Teacher empowerment and autonomy

A professional learning community is enhanced when there is:

- Openness to improvement
- Trust and respect
- A foundation in the knowledge and skills of teaching
- Supportive leadership
- Socialization or school structures that encourage the sharing of the school's vision and mission (Kruse, Louis, & Bryk, 1994)

Source: National School Reform Faculty. (n.d.). Retrieved July 10, 2012, from http://www.nsrfharmony.org.

Professional learning communities (PLCs). As the CFGs took hold at Montgomery, Mrs. O'Brien attended two PLC conferences, led by Rick and Becky DuFour, and brought this framework back to the school. As is their practice, when a new concept is introduced, everyone in the school reads about it, builds common understanding, and then sets out to implement with fidelity. The DuFour definition of a professional learning community is "educators committed to working together using processes of inquiry, problem solving, and reflection upon their practice" (DuFour, 2004; DuFour & Eaker, 1998). The school carefully discerns and adopts the definition and model (see online resources).

The PLC built on the knowledge teachers had gained through Critical Friends dialogue. Using CFG skills of structured, critical reflection, PLCs then introduced team-level analysis of curriculum, instruction, and assessment as it related to individual students and student cohorts. In this way, the model supports teachers developing a deeper sense of content knowledge and vertical alignment, and becoming more transparent with students about the learning goals. Teachers started to set specific, schoolwide, and grade-level goals for student achievement, to consider what it would take for individual teachers to ensure students meet those goals, and to name what special supports and enrichments would be needed. During the PLC process, teachers solidified a commitment to all students doing well, to working together, and understanding specific student achievement needs.

Not all PLCs are built alike. At Montgomery, the setting of SMART (for examples, see Figure 4.3) goals and making them public at the beginning of the school year is an important part of the improvement cycle—the goals are both targets and hypotheses, and the academic year is spent testing out those hypothesis. In this approach, setting high goals is encouraged, even if they are not met, because they facilitate experimentation to get more students learning with greater depth and breadth. These goals are very specific, and they are based on the performance of earlier student cohorts. There is the expectation that the teacher will raise that bar for the next year's class, regardless of the achievement of the incoming class. In this way, goal setting is an exercise in personalizing what each teacher thinks he or she can accomplish the next year. And these goals help teachers to better clarify and articulate what mastery looks like for their students, thus helping teachers pull together to meet these shared team goals. It is about figuring out what each student needs to meet the learning goals, as opposed to customizing the goals for each student.

Figure 4.3   First- and Eighth-Grade Literacy SMART Goals

First Grade

Reading

- By June 2011, 100% of students will score 85% or higher on Treasures Weekly Assessments; these assessment scores may include reteach scores for the first half of the year.
- By June 2011, 100% of students will meet or exceed the target scores for the following assessments:
  o Scholastic Reading Inventory (SRI) (comprehension) as an outcome measure
  o Fountas & Pinnell (comprehension, reading accuracy, fluency) as an outcome measure
  o Students may have their progress monitored on tests that were formerly known as Reading First Assessments, such as DIBELS Oral Reading Fluency (40wpm goal) and/or Gates MacGinitie (44 NCE total reading goal)

Writing

- By June 2011, 100% of students will meet or exceed the expectations for writing:
  o informational report (requiring 3 sentences with relevant details)
  o personal narrative multi-page book
  o response to literary text, as outlined in our Essential Maps for Grade 1
- Response to nonfiction reading as expected by the nonfiction writing
- Rubric for Grade 1expectations (Quarter 1)

Eighth Grade

NECAP

- 93% of students will achieve the standard in reading.
- 100% of students will maintain or exceed their previous achievement level in reading and math.

Reading—Item Bank Assessments

- First Quarter (literary): 65% of students will score 80% or higher.
- Second Quarter (informational): 65% of students will score 80% or higher.
- Third Quarter (literary): 90% of students will score 80% or higher.
- Fourth Quarter (informational): 90% of students will score 80% or higher.

Reading—FNESU Language Arts Assessment (literary and informational texts)

- First Quarter: 65% of students will attain a 3 or above.
- Second Quarter: 75% of students will attain a 3 or above.
- Third Quarter: 85% of students will attain a 3 or above.
- Fourth Quarter: 90% of students will attain a 3 or above, and 80% of students will make a gain of at least one point.

Writing

- 90% of students will score a 3 or better (as assessed by the VT Dept. of Education writing rubrics) on each of the following genres: report, procedure, persuasive, response to literature, narrative, and personal essay.
- 100% of students will maintain or exceed their previous year's score.
- Response to Literary Text (FNESU): 90% of students will achieve a 3 or higher on the district rubric.

Source: Montgomery Center School. Used with permission.

Intervention Strategies

The classroom teacher works with one or more students on particular strategies. Additional approaches include:

- V-math, a 10-module tutorial on key math concepts (working with two to six students)
- Early Reading Support focused on fluency and Fundations
- Special education teacher available for push-in with small group or individual students
- Homework Club, with time at the start and end of the day
- Reteach

Once SMART goals are set and embraced, the PLC structures call for teacher-developed assessments that occur during the instructional cycle. Teachers use these assessments to track progress and to identify which students need additional support and which ones are ready to move forward. Assessments vary from grade to grade, but the multigrade conversations focus on the skills that need to be learned across a grade span, the content that needs to be mastered, and the range of strategies that can support deeper knowledge and mastery, particularly in language arts and mathematics.

At Montgomery, the faculty also drew upon the work of Robert Marzano (2003) to clarify what student mastery looks like, using his nine dimensions of learning, and how to name precise goals, and what research-based instructional strategies to use. Marzano's vocabulary facilitated productive walk-through conversations, according to Mrs. O'Brien. The combination of CFG, which provided protocols and built trust to discuss classroom challenges; the PLC structure of context and focus around data, goal setting, formative assessment, and improvement cycles; and the Marzano constructs around rigor and instruction, led both to rigorous goal setting, and a range of team and individual strategies to achieve those goals. As the faculty became prepared for greater rigor in data analysis, Mrs. O'Brien sought out Reeves Collaborative Consultation as a structure for precise, data discussions (see online resources for sample data analysis template).

While many schools' PLCs can become derailed or flounder because they lack the right conditions (Talbert, 2009), Montgomery demonstrates the precise conditions that Talbert identifies as essential: norms of collaboration, focus on students and their academic performance, access to learning resources for individuals and the group, and mutual accountability for student growth and success. Montgomery's story also corroborates research asserting that achievement gains are met when grade-level teams are provided with the right supports: consistent meeting times, schoolwide instructional leadership, and specific protocols that focus meetings on instructional approaches to students' academic needs (Saunders, Goldenberg, & Gallimore, 2009).

An example: Middle school PLC focus on learners and personalization. Middle school teachers described not needing to focus on basic literacy and numeracy skill building; they are pressing for evidence of critical thinking and complex problem solving. By sixth grade, students have mastery of foundational skills, and the middle school teachers consider it their charge to apply and deepen them, and help students explore deeper understanding of the world and themselves. Within the PLC, literacy, math, and science teachers work with the same students for three years; additional teachers are called upon on an as-needed basis. All teachers are responsible for teaching literacy.

With middle school PLCs, it can be hard to talk about students in a way that encourages each teacher and their students' learning (Mindich & Lieberman, 2012). The Montgomery teachers have sought out ways to help each other: offering support and feedback that is not subject specific; attending standards implementation, rubrics, and how to score them; and organizing resources and strategies to help individual students.

Reteach to personalize learning. At every grade, when instruction and some extra teacher support do not result in students meeting goals, the school uses its reteach model. Initially, every teacher built 30 minutes into each day as the reteach block to support students who have not achieved proficiency on a test. The time is focused on specific skills or knowledge that have not been mastered, or on extending the learning for students who have met the mark. The classroom teacher, assumed to know the students best and having the greatest expertise, works with the students struggling the most, and additional teachers and other resources are brought in to provide support. As the model has evolved, teachers are building reteach strategies into the main part of the school day, modifying and extending them as needed. They are not constrained to a 30-minute block.

This model presses teachers to deeply understand the foundational knowledge that is needed for students to make progress and to either support that learning personally or identify someone else who can. Reteach is meant to deepen teacher understanding of what to look for at each point along the continuum of learning. And as a student attested, it does not assume that students who get good grades know everything, but that all students need a little extra help now and again.

Tracking student progress over time. Progress Toward Meeting the Standards in Math (see Figure 4.4) illustrates how PLCs track the progress of individual students over time (additional tracking resources are available online). Montgomery adapted this form to capture student scores for each quarter, and note strengths and struggles. The largest space on the matrix captures the student's next support, whether he or she is excelling or behind or on target. This places the emphasis on thinking about and attending to what is instructionally next, based on the understanding of student learning in the moment.

This subject-specific reflection happens alongside a big-picture view of each student. The Academic Student Support Team summarizes and documents student strengths and needs (see Figures 4.5 and 4.6) to track the impact of student interventions over time.

The "Interventions to Try" section in Figure 4.6 illustrates Montgomery's assumption that teachers will be experimenting with different approaches to supporting the student, in ongoing pursuit of the right combination of strategies.

Whether it is improving the PLC model, or reteach, or Common Core, teachers at Montgomery experience a range of learning opportunities embedded across the school year (see Table 4.1). They also have time scheduled for their own agenda, more organizational or noninstructional issues. Whole school work addresses schoolwide issues that require common knowledge, capacity, and vertical alignment.

LEADERSHIP AND SYSTEMS SUSTAIN EDUCATOR LEARNING

Beth O'Brien considers herself both a big-picture person and guardian of the bottom line at Montgomery. She also considers it her responsibility to ensure the school's practices have a systemic impact. She talks about helping teachers cultivate habits of mind. For her, these habits come from developing relevant knowledge and practices over the school year and over time, taking up individual reforms and routines that ground and shape the school day and year.

While this sole approach does not necessarily lead to personalization, it describes how cycles of improvement generally take hold. The school's 80% rule focusing on equity and every student doing well requires systems for innovation and improvement to make sure students are known and supported as persons and learners.

Figure 4.4 Progress Toward Meeting the Standards in Math

Grade: _____

Year: _____

Child's Name	Q1	Q2	Q3	Q4	Strengths	Struggles	Next Steps for Instruction/ Learning

Key: a) above level; b) solid on-level; c) shaky on-level; d) nearly achieving; e) below level; f) significantly below level
Identify those students who may benefit from TIER II intervention.

Purpose of the Tool: PLC teams review this sheet, and one for literacy, quarterly.

Unique Use at Montgomery: Multigrade teams use data binders that track specific data sets, providing a big-picture summary, by quarter and student, to plan next steps for instruction.

Source: Beth O'Brien. Used with permission.

Figure 4.5a Academic Student Support Team Form, Page 1

2010–2011 1		Circle Grade K – 1 – 2 – 3

Academic Student Support Team

Student Name: _____   Date: _____

Grade: _____   D.O.B.:_____

Current Teacher:

Support Team:

Follow up Date: Remediation _____ Enrichment _____

                         On Current Plan?   IEP   157   504

Student History

No Previous   Previous   Pre-K ___ K ___ 1 ___ 2 ___
Concerns _____   Referral _____

_____

Identified Areas of Concern (Circle all that apply)

Reading   Spelling   Writing

Math   Speech & Language   Health Concerns

Study/Work Habits   Behavior   V-Math

Summary of Concerns:

Strengths of Child   Needs of Child

Purpose of the Tool:
The Academic Support Team form tracks issues and extra supports provided to individual students.

Unique Use at Montgomery: This two-page form captures previously informal conversations about students' particular needs and strengths, whether for extra help to meet the standards or enrichment for those who are exceeding the standards.

Source: Beth O'Brien. Used with permission.

Figure 4.5b   Academic Student Support Team Form, Page 2

Dates	Accommodations/Interventions	Results or Outcomes

Interventions to Try:

Follow-up Notes:

Source: Beth O'Brien. Used with permission.

Table 4.1 Individual, Team, and Whole School Learning at Montgomery Center School

Individual Learning	Team Learning
Individual Learning Goals Teachers develop individual learning goals that are aligned with schoolwide priorities and student learning data from the previous years. These are reviewed with the principal several times throughout the year. Teachers submit an end-of-year written reflection on their progress, and the principal responds with individual suggestions for next year's learning goals. *Coaching and Modeling* The principal serves as academic coach and strives to visit each teacher's classroom each week. She provides regular descriptive feedback to teachers aligned with their learning goals and schoolwide priorities. *Peer Observations* Each teacher conducts two walk-throughs or peer observations (or one of each) annually. Teachers document how their observations influenced their learning and impacted their instructional practices. *Self-Initiated Learning* Teachers seek out professional learning to attend within and outside of district, as aligned to their individual learning goals and school goals.	*Cross-Grade Teams (PLC)* Multigrade PLC team meetings focus on improving instructional outcomes. Teams set annual SMART goals to establish agreement on broad student learning outcomes. During the year they analyze student assessments and collaboratively examine next steps in learning for individual, small, and whole group instruction. A "general" team meeting also takes place each week to address noninstructional topics. *Team Leadership* Teacher leaders of each multigrade team meet four to five times per year with the principal to review team progress and ensure alignment of efforts across all grades. *Scheduled Team Time* There are three cross-grade teams: preK through 2, grades 3–5, and grades 6–8. Both primary teams (preK–2 and 3–5) meet 90 minutes weekly—45 minutes in PLC time and 45 minutes in general team time. The middle school team meets 1 hour and 45 minutes weekly for PLC time, and 45 minutes every other week for general team time.

Whole School Learning

- Schoolwide learning involves school-level data review, analysis of proposed initiative work, and reflection on implementation of curriculum, instruction, assessment, and behavioral practices.
- Critical Friends Group (CFG) protocols are a primary framework for whole school dialogue, helping to contextualize initiative work in light of existing and effective school practices.
- "Banked time" is used to ensure frequent whole school meeting time. Two full-day professional learning allowances are split to ensure monthly 2.5-hour meetings take place after school, enabling routine analysis and reflection on progress.

Vetting, adopting models with fidelity, and adapting them over time. There is serious intentionality at the school about what models and programs to adopt, when they adopt them, and how they go about implementation over time. Mrs. O'Brien is the undisputed navigator at the school, identifying growth opportunities and capacity building. She says this comes intuitively. She also tracks on reform trends and thinkers nationally, and carefully scouts out and vets resources and programs. Once selected, she brings them to the faculty, and the community immerses themselves.

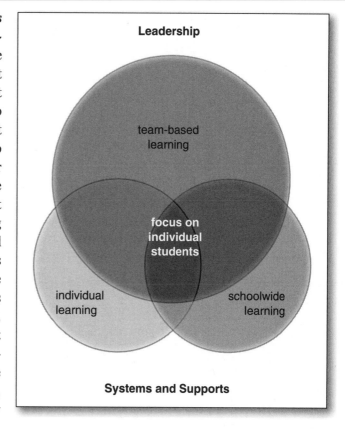

Teachers read and discuss identified books. When the concepts are understood, they are tried out in low-stakes environments.

Mrs. O'Brien does not let the school lurch from one initiative to another. Faculty members don't typically worry about being evaluated on how they implement an initiative in the early stages. Implementation of fidelity over time is the norm, as is the idea the model will evolve. The community makes it their own as a school, and with varying instructional models, the initiative varies among classrooms. The teachers speak about this process of adaptation as routine. Table 4.2 outlines how the range initiatives and outside resources came to the school over time.

"Queen of the forms": principal as guide of routines, protocols, and procedures for continuous improvement. Mrs. O'Brien unabashedly explains her love of routines and protocols, and the templates and forms that go with them. She has even dubbed herself "Queen of the Forms." For her, forms focus and structure opportunities for reflection and dialogue, and press for the development of specific habits of mind. Mrs. O'Brien speaks to drawing on many different resources to find forms

Table 4.2 Professional Learning Over Time at Montgomery Center School

Journey in Professional Learning to Personalize Student Learning, 2002–2012		
2002–2005	**2006–2009**	**2010–2012**
Principal and lead teachers participate in Critical Friends training to learn protocols. Full school learns from them and starts use of protocols. This laid the groundwork for developing PLCs. Teachers pair up as Critical Friends partners; to dialogue about "issues of practice," integrated "Looking at Student Work" protocols in faculty meetings, which provided a launch point for additional data-analysis protocols. Principal restructures professional learning time to ensure faculty learning across the year, and to have ongoing time for book studies and Critical Friends meeting time.	Advanced Critical Friends training is provided through National School Reform Faculty for PLC team leaders to develop additional dialogue and leadership skills. Teachers and principal participate in learning walks together, in order to develop consistent instructional practices and to provide additional opportunities for peer dialogue. Faculty members integrate regular use of root cause analysis, which helped reframe student learning needs from a deficit-based approach to learning (what don't students know) to a strengths-based approach to learning.	Teachers conduct walk-throughs and peer observations on their own. Teachers lead PLC team meetings and are supported to ensure consistent schoolwide practices through quarterly team leader meetings with the principal.
Capacity to reflect on practice, conduct observations, and offer feedback		
Dip in math scores reveals strength in math skills but not application of skills. This catalyzed reassignment of teachers, adoption of Mathland and Bridges math programs. Faculty focuses on building literacy skills through nonfiction and literacy across the content areas	Reading First grant (2006–08) brings more structured focus on literacy and vertical alignment, and data analysis related to literacy. Book study: *Classroom Instruction That Works: Research-Based Strategies for Increasing Student Achievement* (Marzano, Pickering, & Pollock, 2001). Faculty spends three years on this book study. They build common vocabulary regarding instruction and research-based learning strategies, establish schoolwide expectations for use of consistent instructional practice, and develop foundation for learning walks practice.	Book study: *The Art and Science of Teaching: A Comprehensive Framework for Effective Instruction* (Marzano, 2007). Study guides effective note taking, organizing content into manageable chunks, and developing specific engagement strategies. Book study: *Focus: Elevating the Essentials to Radically Improve Student Learning* (Schmoker, 2011). Principal supports intentional lesson planning using Madeline Hunter format, and strategies for incorporating authentic literacy across the content. Faculty works on understanding and initial implementation of Common Core, developing strategies for argumentative writing and deep reading in all content areas.
Capacity to develop and deliver curriculum and instruction		

that the school uses, but then always modifies them over time "to make them our own." This is not just a penchant for matrices and checklists, but a strategy for personalizing professional learning. Drawing from outside resources, she recasts them considering her faculty's (or a teacher or team's) prior knowledge and current needs, and frames rich content in a way that will be accessible and challenge colleagues to reach their latest goals.

She develops habits for student goal setting and routines for ensuring that each student is meeting them. This cycle is framed by the annual schedule: setting SMART goals in early fall, developing the range of strategies to employ, and attending to the effective functioning of the PLC—a combination of documented expectations for what PLCs will deliver as a team, how individual teachers will approach their reteach plan, and additional staff providing instructional supports and interventions.

Systems in small schools. Even though there is debate about whether small school size correlates with higher achievement, small teacher-student ratios create instant envy for the high school teacher responsible for 150 students. Well-run small classes lend themselves to conferencing, for students giving voice to their ideas in the full class, and community building.

Small school size also presents systemic challenges. There are fewer teachers to rotate through bus duty, to be on different committees, to be leaders of professional learning, which can divert teacher energies outside the classroom to administrative tasks and away from the craft of teaching. To maximize the school's success, Mrs. O'Brien seeks out and cultivates teachers flexible about their teaching assignments and eager to learn with others.

Heat and Light 5

Tusculum View Elementary School (PreK–5), Greeneville, Tennessee

> *A fourth-grade boy arrives new to school. He is reading at first-grade level. The special education teacher scaffolds his learning supports and works with the classroom teacher so he can be in the regular education classroom. Yet he shows no interest in reading. After months, he one day stands by her shoulder as she does a read aloud. He comes alive with a story about airplanes and aircraft carriers. The teacher recognizes the moment. She immediately taps her grade-level team and the librarian to help locate high-interest, leveled books on aviation. Together, the educators also develop additional reading strategies to support him. How else to seize the moment? The school has high school student mentors who are in the Reserve Officers Training Corps (ROTC). The special education teacher seeks out one who loves airplanes, and pairs up the mentor with the boy. They read together weekly, and become fast friends. A year later, the boy had made more than one year's progress.*

These classes in the school's sprawling, open-space layout represent the energy and activity present throughout. Students and teachers are aware of their next steps in learning. Pat Donaldson, a seasoned special education teacher from the school and its principal since 2008, says, "Teachers here have always believed that you take kids where they are; whoever comes we try to zero in on that child's need." Based on this value, teachers "take [the student] from this step to the next step, whatever that step is." For several years, the school has focused on these next steps, and helping students know how to take them with increasing precision. The school values both the light that comes with an excitement to learn, opportunities, supports, and flexibility, and the heat of high standards and accountability. Both work in symbiosis to continuously deepen and accelerate student progress.

SUPPORTING INDIVIDUALIZED LEARNING FOR STUDENTS AND TEACHERS

The faculty sets specific, short-term, individual goals with students and helps them move at their own pace, in the way they each learn best. One third-grade teacher explains, "It started with differentiating. It was never not present. Our district put a focus on it, and our school is very proactive. We talk about where we are headed in the longer term." Holly Ward, the ELL coordinator, puts it this way: "Differentiated instruction is not a new thing that we will just add to our bookshelf. It is something we are becoming; it is a part of who we are."

The educators in the school are committed to rallying to help each other, students and staff, including the school counselor, Angie Shelton. Mrs. Shelton, who had learned about and developed Social Stories, writes booklets for and about individual students. The booklets have photos and descriptions of situations where the student behaves well and how the student should act in a certain situation. Adapting the social story idea for some primary students who don't yet read, the school counselor approaches Pat Fay, the school's media specialist and librarian, with the idea of making Social Stories as videos. Together they integrate video of students caught in the act of being good, with narration reinforcing appropriate and calming behaviors. The video is downloaded on computers in the classrooms, and when a student is out of

---

Tusculum View Elementary School

Demographics and Commendations

Number of Students: 352
Percentage Eligible for Free and Reduced-Price Lunch: 45.9%
Percentage of Limited English Proficient: 6%
Percentage of Special Education: 14%
Racial/Ethnic Percentages:

- Hispanic: 9.7%
- Black: 6.1%
- White: 80.9%
- Asian/Pacific Island: 3.3%

Sampling of Commendations:

- Blue Ribbon Lighthouse School—2011
- Tennessee Reward School recognizing high achievement and continuous growth—2012
- USDA Healthy Schools Award—2012

Source: Tennessee Department of Education (n.d.). Report card: State assessment results (search by school). Retrieved from http://edu.reportcard.state.tn.us/pls/apex/f?p=200:30:3324460927197276::NO

sorts, the teacher may suggest that he or she take a few minutes to watch their personalized video. This has grown to six videos in kindergarten through fourth grades, plus 25 Social Stories as booklets. And other students are asking for videos about them, too. Explains Mrs. Shelton, "I like to come up with wonderful ideas but I don't necessarily know how to do them. . . . [For this to work,] you had to have a tech person who is very helpful, teachers willing to try it, and a principal who will let you do it."

Teams are expected to implement what they have learned from workshops in order to implement system-level goals. Grade-level teams apply the new skills and customize strategies for particular students. The first-grade team describes its focus on mathematics achievement when scores declined several years ago as follows:

> **Thinkers and Texts That Influence Tusculum View**
>
> - Victoria Bernhardt, *Data Analysis for Continuous School Improvement* (2004)
> - Carol Ann Tomlinson, *The Differentiated Classroom: Responding to the Needs of All Learners* (1999)
> - Ron Berger, *An Ethic of Excellence: Building a Culture of Craftsmanship With Students* (2003)
> - Alan Blankstein, *The Answer Is in the Room: How Effective Schools Scale Up Student Success* (2011)
> - Douglas Reeves, *Transforming Professional Development Into Student Results* (2010) and *The Learning Leader: How to Focus School Improvement for Better Results* (2006)
> - Wade Boykin and Pedro Noguera, *Creating the Opportunity to Learn: Moving From Research to Practice to Close the Achievement Gap* (2011)

Mrs. Hoese   The math workshops we have been to in the last two years on DI [Differentiated Instruction] . . . have been absolutely wonderful. We don't always come up with our new ideas. You get things and we can build from that.

Mrs. Stearns   Our workshops were all hands on. They had it set up so we could go to each of the learning centers and see the different ways to differentiate for different learners.

Mrs. Hoese   We actually made the activity for a sample, and that's what I'm doing now. I'm creating three classroom sets. . . . If we make one set we make one for all three. And that's what my parent volunteer is doing today. It's a math activity she is doing for DI that she is doing for all three classes.

Mrs. Stearns   I actually thought I was a very good math teacher. Karen and I both attended Math Their Way, and Box and Bag It, some of the older ones that have such great value to them. And so when we got with these [district] math consulting folks, they kind of took that and updated it, and brought in some new ideas.

Mrs. Hoese   Stacy [the school-based, academic coach] is taking, in addition to our regular series, and the math workshops we've been to, all the different parts and assembling them together by topics from all the different PDs [professional development sessions] that we've had; she's organizing them by topic.

Mrs. Stearns   She's aligning all the activities we've been given. . . . So she's aligning it to all of our lessons. . . . She'll go out and hunt and bring [resources] back to us so that we have something to work with, to meet the needs of different students. I've got a student who does fourth-grade math. I needed something else for him. I had stuff up to third grade, but I did not have anything for fourth. So she went out . . .

When a goal is set, the district mobilizes a range of resources such as coaches or instructional materials, and offers them in a way that is accessible to teachers with varied experience. There are supports at the school level to help teachers integrate and use these skills collaboratively to improve practice.

A RURAL SCHOOL WITH A TRACK RECORD

Tusculum View Elementary School (Tusculum View) is nestled in the Smokey Mountains, the part of Appalachia that is Northeastern Tennessee. The community has risen to high academic ranks in the Greeneville City Schools and state. The district is high performing within the state, which was early to garner federal Race to the Top (RTTT) funding. Tusculum View has had a persistent track record of high achievement across subgroups, particularly over the past six years. (See Figure 5.1 for 2011–2012 subgroup achievement scores). The school opened in 1967 with a progressive agenda for student-centered learning, and there is a tradition of attracting those who are interested in innovation, and who are comfortable with collaboration. The meaning of learning and collaboration has evolved substantially over time, and has required vigilant attention.

Figure 5.1 Tusculum View Elementary School State Assessment, 2011-2012 Subgroup Comparison

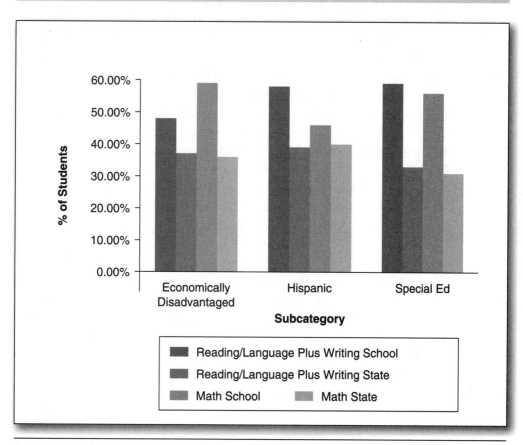

Source: Tennessee Department of Education, http://edu.reportcard.state.tn.us/pls/apex/f?p=200:1: 2927432404018901:NO (retrieved December 1, 2012).

Attending to Equity and Honoring Changing Demographics

Increasing differentiation for each student increasingly means keeping an equity agenda front and center. Over the past 10 years, Tusculum View has gone from being almost completely Caucasian to having 10% Hispanic and 6% African American students, with both of those populations continuing to grow. Families of these children are physicians, migrant workers, educators, police officers, truck drivers, nail salon workers, airline pilots, fast-food workers, and stay-at-home moms. Some are unemployed. Three percent of students are from Japan and are at the school for a few years while a parent works on location at a nearby Japanese firm. The school enrolls some of the area's wealthiest students and some of its poorest. Some families from other towns pay to enroll their students at Tusculum View because they value the education and the diversity. "We are proud of our diversity. We talk about it in newsletters. Photos deliberately represent diversity. Music and art programs focus on that. We would love to have more diversity of teachers. This is hard in a small, rural area. Many student teachers of color don't choose to stay in the area."

Mrs. Donaldson does not abide any suggestion that economics, language, or race might change the school's current track record on students' achievement. "I have been pretty vocal about attitudes and about what we can change, what we have control of, and what we don't have control of." With professional learning, that has translated into the school doing a book study on Jensen's *Teaching With Poverty in Mind: What Being Poor Does to Kids' Brains and What Schools Can Do About It* (2009). Mrs. Donaldson makes this required reading for any new teacher who comes to the school. "As our economically disadvantaged population grows, I think it is important for us to keep a positive focus on what we as a school can change." To improve faculty understanding about students, families, and the community, Mrs. Donaldson has facilitated schoolwide outreach, particularly to unfamiliar neighborhoods:

> We have actually been out in our community. We went out the year before last with bags of cookies to the apartments here and the trailer park to welcome students and families to a new school year. . . . We rode a regular school bus and took our students' bus routes to see where some of our children come from. We are trying to do things, actually taking some of our parenting classes into those neighborhoods and trying to connect with families and offer supports to them.

Mrs. Donaldson encourages compassion and understanding about everyone in "our community," and is paying particular attention to students whose backgrounds and demographics are new to the school, whose backgrounds are different from those of the staff. She presses for this knowledge about personal context as another data point in the reach for high standards.

JUST-IN-TIME SUPPORTS FOR TEACHERS

Pat Fay's time as media specialist and school librarian is organized around responding to teacher requests and needs. "I support individual teachers as they have ideas about what they want to implement. . . . The message from the district and then the school is: learning is first, and technology supports that." Mrs. Fay thinks a lot about the pacing of support. She looks to offer "just enough, just in time. . . . We don't want to give them too much, it overwhelms them." Mrs. Fay offers some workshops for the school and district, but she largely responds to individual requests for support. For example, she is currently collaborating with a first-grade teacher to develop virtual student portfolios.

Coaching also exemplifies "just-in-time" support. The district launched the academic coaching initiative with an eye to building school capacity systemically, providing Reading Specialist Mia Hyde, who currently supports integrating the Common Core with language arts work; District Data Coach Brandy Shelton, who facilitates a newly formed data team and helps make meaning of a range of data; and 13-year veteran elementary teacher Stacy King became full-time academic coach two and one-half years ago. Mrs. King has professional strength in math content and pedagogy, and is working with other academic coaches to deepen her understanding of change, data use, professional dialogue, and adult learning. She has built relationships and collaborated effectively, always supporting improvement by scouting out the right resources for teachers. Mrs. Stearns, from the first grade, says,

> Our Stacy King has been absolutely—it's like having a diamond. It's like we've each been given a diamond. I hope they never take away that position. . . . As much as I was questioning it at the beginning, I don't know how we could do without it. . . . There's no money to send everyone to the workshops. So if you send one good one to the workshop and she presents it to our kids and presents it to us . . .

A third-grade teacher describes Mrs. King and her work this way: "She is not just any coach. She is stellar. . . . I think of Stacy as a filter. She gets all this information. She filters out the things that don't apply to us, and she gives us what we need." Mrs. King explains her approach this way: "As we got into differentiated instruction for students, we said, 'If we ask them to do it, then we have to do it [for teachers].'" She goes on, "I am having to think about where each individual teacher is. I think about their growth plan, finding additional resources." She is also conscientious about giving teachers flexibility: "I really want them to have options so that [they] can make educated decisions about the instruction they are planning for their students."

As with Mrs. Fay and Mrs. Shelton, Mrs. King in general does not work with teachers or teams unless they ask. At first, it took some time to build trust. "Some wanted me to move into their classrooms, others not. This year, [educator] evaluations systems have framed how I offer support. Most have written me into their growth plan."

There is an exception to this rule: When teachers are placed at Stage 1 using the new state evaluation system, it means they need the most intense level of support, and district policy dictates that all new teachers receive Stage 1 support. Teachers may also be at Stage 1 as the result of the supervision and evaluation process. Teachers at Stage 1 are required to work with coaches, and Mrs. King helps them with lesson planning, thinking through student groupings and instructional strategies, with content and data expertise. Her overall approach is the same as with every teacher: She looks "at their need at the moment, within the realm of looking at student self-assessment, formative assessment, and differentiation—the current school priorities."

Individualized Teacher Learning in Context

Mrs. King and Mrs. Donaldson work as a team to base professional learning on teacher needs and strengths as they relate to student learning. Mrs. Donaldson sees her role this way:

> It's my job to be in tune enough with my staff to know where the needs are. Stacy and I work very closely to make sure that teachers get what they need. Stacy is more hands on. If they need time, if they need money, if they need supplies, that's my job.

There are required state and district reforms to consider as well. "Many times we don't have a choice. With Common Core we don't have choices. It's here and [the teachers] understand that." Mrs. Donaldson says, "Balancing school and district professional development is always a challenge. There's a need to balance. . . . I personally feel that teachers' professional development needs to be differentiated in the same way that student learning is." So the leaders filter and contextualize these requirements in a way that honors where the school and individual teachers are, and what they need next. "A key to any of our professional development is seeing how it applies to our work, and having time to work on that," Mrs. King explains.

"There are [district] expectations and requirements, but then schools do have discretion. The assistant director for instruction [at the central office] was helpful in allowing me in changing our schedule; the other elementary school schedules don't look like ours," Mrs. Donaldson notes as she reflect on the district role. She and Mrs. King discern how to meet district standards and sync up district requirements and school-based priorities, and are in dialogue with district staff about how the initiatives can work in their context. At the same time, they also egg on district innovations. "Our school pushes on the district expectations. It is a philosophy. We are not satisfied. We are always hungry," says Mrs. Donaldson.

Mrs. King and Mrs. Donaldson talk about substantial shifts that took place when there was anticipation of math scores dipping districtwide three years ago, and the development of their change strategy:

Mrs. Donaldson   The change in schedule [was made] to get more instructional time in math. . . . There was some moving around of teachers so that I felt I had the best people for the fourth and fifth grade [classrooms].

Mrs. King   They were moved to work in their best areas of strength. We wanted to put them where their strengths were.

Mrs. Donaldson   [We rethought] the amount of professional development, and how we did professional development in math. The system provided Marie and Tammy [content and instructional experts]. Stacy [school-based, academic coach] redelivered and worked alongside those teachers. She did [voluntary] after-school study groups and they [the teachers] all came.

Mrs. King   We actually started before Tammy and Marie. I went to a regional NCTM [National Council of Teachers of Mathematics] conference and attended some sessions led by Kim Sutton. The way she thought about math had an impact on me. I said, "This is the missing piece for us." Even before we changed the schedule, I started working with teachers. Mrs. Donaldson gave me access to purchase many of the materials that Kim Sutton had developed. I actually did after school [study groups], not only with our school but invited other schools, too. I knew that we had to do something different in math. We were doing skills in isolation and not seeing the connections, and that was very apparent. That got us started. . . . Teachers began talking about math and why we were doing it the way we were.

Mrs. Donaldson	It was a schoolwide effort. It wasn't just the fourth- and fifth-grade teachers where students were involved in high-stakes testing.
Mrs. King	That was special.
Mrs. Donaldson	We wanted everyone thinking about math and how we teach math.
Mrs. King	It was a combination of all of it. Our scores have to improve. We made adjustments. . . . It took guts. Everyone was not happy about it and did not know if it was going to work. We had to convince them that it was going to work. We had to convince them.

What's challenging in these instances for the principal? "Worrying about holding up the vision for the teachers and what we need to accomplish, and not killing them in the process." Having a very self-motivated staff gives the principal's work a particular twist. "The teachers are type A. If I'm not pushing, they are pushing. They are driving themselves. And just how to keep that balance there . . . that's the hardest thing for me."

Most teachers are propelled by both internal motivation and the success they have experienced. Mrs. Fay has come to expect that requests for help will lead to broader innovation or improvement. "If one team member uses something a lot, the rest of the team will get on board." Mrs. King and Mrs. Donaldson want to capitalize on this professional energy without depleting it, so they are continuously considering the pacing, spacing, and scaffolding of initiatives, and the learning that is necessary to embed these practices.

> Mrs. Donaldson identifies practices helpful for this process: Talking with Stacy and having a real pulse on where the teachers are, and when I might need to step back and when I need to push more. Knowing what's going on with my staff personally, what's going on in their personal lives also informs that. Talking with other leaders in the school, other principals, other people I respect.

Collaboration Developing Over Time

Coaches and teachers collaborate primarily in grade-level teams, a strategy deliberately cultivated through professional learning design. Mrs. Donaldson speaks to the change,

Five or six years ago the professional development was "sit and get," and now we know PD can be done in a better way. We feel like allowing teachers to work with each other more is more appropriate and beneficial for teachers professionally, and for student achievement. Within the [grade] teams, teachers are sharing with each other. . . . Teachers grading each other's [students'] work, beginning to build some exemplars.

Nowadays, the teams are the first place teachers go to troubleshoot, get ideas for instruction, understand data, and figure out the next right step for moving a student forward. Third grade is a case in point. Third-grade teacher Amy Haynie comments,

We work very closely with our team. We could not live without them. We take turns. We divide our workload. . . . The majority of our conversations are "this afternoon, next week, this kid is doing this." Or, "Let's go over this concept. I need to pull a group to reteach this lesson."

Conversations focus on student outcomes, using data, sharing resources, applying new content knowledge. Third-grade teachers talk about this year's focus: student self-assessment and goal-setting. Mrs. Haynie continues, "We use our discretion. We think about that child. Are they a fast or slow reader? Is the score accurate?" Teachers confer with students at least weekly to better understand their level of achievement. Melanie Williams adds, "We look at STAR [benchmark] reading and STAR math goals and say, 'This is where you started. This is where proficient is' and then we engage them in goal setting." A teacher may suggest a nine-week goal, "and the students often say 'I can do more than that.'" In this process, teachers tell students "no goals are better or worse. We all have our strengths." The goals live alongside specific instructional practices that reflect deep content, support within and after school, particular texts and other resources that may help, and advice on how to work with individual students. As Mrs. Donaldson points out, the teachers "don't just conference with students who are having a problem; they conference with *every* student." The third-grade team decided to focus on this together. Mrs. Williams explains their common professional development goal:

We chose student self-assessments, and then we've been using Stacy to help with that. We've developed some on our own weekly assessments. Stacy shared it with us. Then teachers were talking about a website they found with a checklist. . . . This is a natural next step for where we're going. It's an extension off of differentiation.

What's Next for Team Capacity?

Mrs. King works to be in the moment when helping teachers to be reflective, responding to teacher needs, while having a sense of direction for professional learning. The next horizon is in sight:

> We have common planning. We want them to take what they're doing with their teams to the next level to where it truly impacts and they're making decisions about individual kids as a team. We say we're collaborative, and we are. But there's a difference between working in the same room together and even planning [instruction] together, and truly making decisions about kids based on what's going on in the classroom from one day to another. Those are our next steps. We continue to refine our work with formative assessments, student self-assessment, and base our decisions on the needs of individual students and how to move them to the next level. We have moved from grade-level planning, to a model, in fourth and fifth grades, where teachers meet as a leadership team once a week with an agenda to discuss student needs (academic, behavior, attendance, etc.) and how to address these needs as a team.

She and Mrs. Donaldson also hear the clock ticking. From the beginning, everyone has known the coaching position is time bound, and based on external funding. How does this make them think about the work? Mrs. King explains, "We went into this wanting teachers to coach each other. I'm hoping that through the work I've done with teachers, I hope we're at a place where they are coaching each other—to get to the place where it is not just working to impact teachers, but to impact students. It just does not happen overnight."

ANALYSIS

Working together, Mrs. Donaldson as principal and Mrs. King as academic coach personalize professional learning, mirroring the ideals of the classroom: helping learners understand and be responsible for goals; exchanging help with peers; understanding the own styles, capacities, and interests; and continuously tracking their progress. They ground capacity building in positive supports and affirmations they consider to be the "light": opportunities to encourage self-motivated individuals and teams, making room for innovation and mistakes in the name of learning, and supporting individual teachers and teams. These opportunities and supports are not simply let loose, but tempered and given boundaries by "heat": high expectations that are vigorously tracked, with directive supports and interventions activated by unmet expectations. Mrs. Donaldson and Mrs. King attend to the right balance of light and heat. Values are the foundation for this work.

SCHOOL VALUES MADE EXPLICIT AND VISIBLE

Know yourself, and keep learning. Both adults and children actively reflect on their knowledge and skills, likes, dislikes, and inclinations. Identifying issues and pursuing solutions is organic and constructivist, following the National Research Council's (2000) work, which asserts that metacognitive capacity is one of our most important abilities: mapping existing knowledge and discerning how to extend and deepen it.

Foster success with practice and support. The community puts hard work ahead of smarts. Learning is more successful when people commit to tasks, invest effort, and persevere. Learners are guided to their appropriate level of challenge and know it is their responsibility to make the effort required to achieve mastery. Mistakes become part of the learning journey rather than being a source of embarrassment or punishment, following Carol Dweck's (2006) work on mindsets, which suggests that learning is not based on a fixed, prior ability, but is fluid and dynamic when there is purposeful engagement, challenge, and effort.

Support learning, just enough, just in time. Everyone has different talents and learning styles, and their need for help varies in amount, content, style, and timing. Educators are responsible for scaffolding that supports learners where they are.

Principal's Vision

It is my vision that Tusculum View is a place where students and teachers grow to their personal best, academic excellence is achieved, habits and values for successful living are developed, and the school, home, and community partner to ensure every child's success.

Balance light and heat. Supports and encouragement are balanced with high standards and a challenge to do well. This balance is as important to the principal and coach as it is to teachers helping students pace themselves through rigorous standards and lessons. When teachers or students don't rise to high standards naturally, more supports are provided, building on Elmore's (2000) assertion that for every additional level of expectations placed on teachers, there should be corresponding supports.

PROFESSIONAL LEARNING FOCUSES ON EACH STUDENT AS A PERSON AND A LEARNER

Building Understanding of Students to Shape the Learning Experience

To start the year, every Tusculum View student completes an interest survey outlining their favorite activities and what they want to learn more about. In lower grades, the questions are framed to elicit interesting responses; for example, "What is one thing that I want everyone to know about me?" In later years, students are asked for more detailed information, including what they want to learn more about, how they learn, their hobbies, extracurricular interests, and what would make school interesting for them. See web resources for an example of the fifth-grade Student Interview and Parent Interview templates. Beyond general interest, some surveys probe more specifically about students as learners (see Figure 5.2).

Differentiation to Engage Students as Learners

Differentiation is a prime strategy for personalized learning, drawing on Carol Ann Tomlinson's (1999) work on student readiness, interests, and preferred ways of learning. Differentiated lesson planning—teaching "up"—starts with setting high-level goals and then creating the right scaffolds for each student to reach them.

Teachers design lesson plans using student inventories. Figure 5.3 is a unit organizer that shows choices for each unit, and different ways to organize reflection and analysis. Drawing from Tomlinson's model, the unit plan identifies student learning goals in the form of "I can" statements. Students use this plan with teachers to clarify goals and to think about how they want to achieve them.

Figure 5.2 Fifth-Grade Fall Reading Interview

Name: _____ Date: _____

1. Do you like to read? _____
   Why or why not?
   _____
   _____

2. *About* how many books did you read last year?
   _____

3. How often do you read at home?
   _____

4. What books have you read recently?
   _____
   _____

5. What do you do when something doesn't make sense?
   _____
   _____
   _____

6. What do you do when you come to a word you have trouble
   reading?
   _____
   _____
   _____

7. How do you feel when you are reading out loud?
   _____

8. What kinds of texts do you like to read?
   ____ fiction picture books   ____ chapter books
   ____ magazines   ____ nonfiction   ____ poetry

9. Do you think reading is hard or easy for you? _____
   Why? _____
   _____

10. Where is your favorite place to read? _____

Purpose of the Tool:
This survey seeks to understand the students' personal interests in reading as well as how they learn as readers.

Unique Use at Tusculum View: Interest survey results are administered at the beginning of the year and shared within the team setting, so that all grade-level teachers learn about the passions and interests of each student. Teachers are motivated to exchange these types of inventories with one another, and with the coach, who may also help circulate examples of these tools to teachers across the school, and more important, who can speak to how their use is applied, point to specific examples of use in the school, and direct an interested teacher to another colleague.

Source: Carla Renner. Teacher, Tusculum View Elementary School. Used with permission.

Figure 5.3 Fifth-Grade 5 Unit Organizer

Tusculum View Grade 5

Name: _____

Genre: Biography (Artists)

Skill: Author's Purpose and Fact and Opinion

Weeks of: 12/6/11 – 12/16/11

Vocabulary Practice

Complete ONE activity to complete with your List 9 vocabulary words.

- Make an illustrated dictionary for all vocabulary terms.
- Write a journal entry using all vocabulary words from the perspective of a character of your choice.
- Make up a song, poem, cheer, or picture that represents your vocabulary terms and meanings.

Comprehension Practice

Author's Purpose (to inform, to entertain, to persuade, to share feelings, and to describe)

Start activity on 12/8/11

Independent Activity

Write a paragraph on each form of author's purpose. One paragraph should inform, one to entertain, one to persuade, one to share feelings, and one to describe. It is your choice on what the paragraph is about. ☺

Comprehension Practice

Fact and Opinion/Reality and Fantasy

Start activity on 12/12/11

Independent Activity

Choose a topic of your choice. Provide 5 facts and 5 opinions about the topic.

Example:

Topic: Fantasy

Opinion: Fantasy books are the best stories to read.

Fact: Harry Potter is the genre of fantasy.

Reading

Reader's Response

Write a reader's response letter to me in your reader's response notebook using your "just right book." Your question from me for this letter is: **What is the author's purpose? What did the author have to know in order to write this story?** Remember to look at your guidelines in the front of your reader's response notebook.

Leveled Reader Activity With Ms. Renner

Activity on 12/13/11

Using one of the leveled readers (Da Vinci's Designs, Michelangelo and the Italian Renaissance, or The Inspiration of Art) determine the importance of the text with a three-column FQR.

Writing Practice

Start paper on 12/7/11

Write a five-paragraph essay (use a flow map for prewriting), using the prompt below. Remember, each paragraph (beginning, 3 middles, and conclusion) should be at least 5-7 sentences.

Prompt: Pretend that one of the paintings in our "classroom museum" comes to life as you are admiring it. Write about what happens next. Please write this essay on loose-leaf notebook paper and NOT in your writer's notebook. Remember to keep your essay focused, organized, and with a lot of figurative language. Also remember to not over use dialogue.

Please do some form of prewriting to organize your thoughts.

Please remember to use transitional phrases, embedded transitions, appropriate usage of dialogue, a grabber lead, a great ending, and Show Me, Don't Tell Me.

I Can:

____ Identify the author's purpose (i.e., to inform, to entertain, to share feelings, to describe, to persuade).

____ Distinguish between fact/opinion and reality/fantasy.

____ Organize, develop, and write at least 5 paragraphs using topic sentences and supporting details.

Source: Carla Renner, Teacher, Tusculum View Elementary School. Used with permission.

Formative Assessment to Help Students Name
Their Learning and Recognize Next Steps

Formative assessment progresses naturally from differentiation, as teachers become more precise about each student's needs, and how to measure and pace learning to close achievement gaps.

Prior to implementing formative assessment, using a nine-week benchmark assessment cycle, teachers and students set learning goals against which to measure growth. The second grade is tracking on six reading units over the academic year (see Figure 5.4).

As formative assessment is introduced, all grades have begun to implement weekly student self-assessments as a frequent and targeted opportunity for reflection, conferring with students, and planning next instructional steps. Drawing on data to inform next steps, teachers are developing proficiency in teaching students, rather than being flummoxed by the data, or leaping to use strategies without knowing how they connect to students' styles, abilities, and skills. Formative data tells educators whether students have mastered a skill or "not yet." (For an example of a student checklist, see Figure 5.5).

Both differentiation and formative assessment require that teachers know students as persons and learners. Team meetings provide a forum to provide personalized student support, and address both the planning and implementation of this work. Over time, teacher teams select student groups, organize to provide one-on-on instruction, develop centers, define reteaching needs, provide enrichment for those who are ready, and recraft lesson plans to differentiate results based on student learning needs. Using evidence of learning to plan for next steps in instruction is becoming part of the culture. Professional learning supports include the district data coach, who is available to support individual and team understanding of benchmark and summary data. The district reading specialist, data coach, and the school-based academic coach are ready to help understand content-specific implications of data, formulate next instructional steps, and guide student responsibility for their own learning.

Reflection: In your school, what is being done to help teachers use a wide range of assessment data to guide and personalize daily instruction? How are students involved in setting goals based on data?

Figure 5.4   Second-Grade Reading Growth Charts

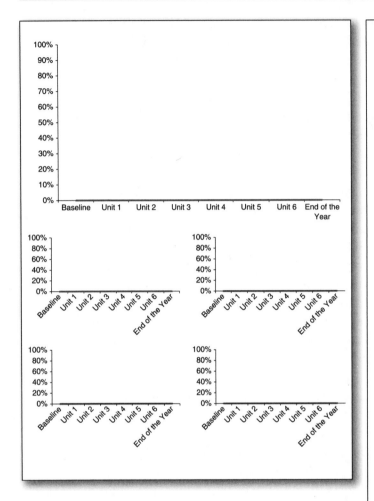

Purpose of the Tool: This chart captures reading growth for each student by tracking the scores of each unit test. It tracks phonic, comprehension, vocabulary, and grammar, and the large graph illustrates the composite reading score.

Unique Use at Tusculum View: Grade-level teams each use a chart to support individual teacher conferencing with students about their progress in each area of reading. The student graphs a score for phonics, comprehension, vocabulary, and grammar. At the beginning of the year, the teacher and student together graph the baseline test and discuss reading goals for the year. As the year continues, they confer about if the goals are being met and whether new goals should be set. In doing this, the students have a realistic grasp of the growth they have made throughout the year. It also creates the opportunity to discuss what can support skill development: helpful tools, resources, extended time on task, or texts—or the use of additional supports beyond the classroom.

Source: Tusculum View Elementary School Second Grade Team. Used with permission.

Figure 5.5 Third-Grade Paragraph Writing Self-Assessment

State Standard: Write in complete sentences developed into a logical, coherent paragraph with a topic sentence, supporting details, and a concluding sentence.

Question	Yes	Not Yet
Did I indent the first line of my paragraph?		
Did I include a clear topic sentence?		
Did I include at least 3 good detail sentences to support my topic sentence?		
Did I include a closing sentence that tells how I feel about the topic?		
Did I use good describing words to form a picture in my readers' minds?		
Do my sentences begin with capital letters?		
Do my sentences end with the correct punctuation?		
Did I reread my work to make sure that all of my sentences make sense?		

Student Comments: _____

_____

Teacher Comments: _____

_____

Purpose of the Tool: The weekly student checklist allows for student self-reflection. It encourages students to consider what they have done well and what they need to do next.

Unique Use at Tusculum View: This type of checklist frames weekly conferencing between the teacher and students. The format underscores that learning is ongoing, and that in time, students will in fact use each of the key writing elements. It's just "not yet" reflected in the current piece of work. The space below allows for reflection on what's next.

Source: Adapted from Kay Burke materials presented to Greeneville Public Schools, 2012.

Professional learning to support differentiation and formative assessment, and for other priorities, is a combination of schoolwide, team-based, and individual efforts (see Table 5.1). The next section of this analysis provides a deeper description of how these ideas take hold and are integrated in a systemic framework.

Table 5.1 Individual, Team, and Whole School Learning at Tusculum View Elementary School

Individual Learning	Team Learning
Individual Learning Goals Each educator sets individual learning goals each year, based on schoolwide goals and priorities and aligned with personal interests. Teacher learning goals are used to guide coaching, modeling, and reflection sessions with coaches, and are discussed with teams so that peers can support colleagues' improvement. *Coaching and Modeling* The academic coach provides a range of supports including model lessons, teacher observations with feedback, and classroom observations with feedback. District coaches in reading and data use work with teachers during team time and also in the classroom setting. *Peer Observations* Peer observations are encouraged and take place to deepen schoolwide expectations related to data use, differentiation, and formative assessment. Feedback from these sessions is largely informal. *Self-Initiated Learning* Self-initiated learning most often happens at the team level and is driven by both individual teacher passion and the school's annual priorities.	*Grade-Level Team* Teams work is organized using an informal inquiry cycle that involves continuous analysis and review of learning goals, instruction, and assessment. Teams • review benchmark data; • establish learning outcomes; • develop daily assessments; • review daily assessment data; • sharpen learning goals for each—student and for groups of students based on data; and • plan how to differentiate instruction. *Vertical Teams* In grades 4 and 5, teachers meet weekly both in grade-level teams and also in multigrade content teams. *Data Team* There is a school data team that is led by the district data coach. This team primarily reviews benchmark data to analyze schoolwide trends. *Scheduled Team Time* Grade teams have scheduled time to meet one hour per week, though all teams meet more frequently than that. The schedule allows for teams to meet for one hour daily if they choose.

Whole School Learning

• Schoolwide priorities are the driver for team and individual learning through the course of a school year.
• Schoolwide priorities and goals are largely determined by district initiatives; most recently that included differentiation, student self-assessment practices, student conferencing, and use of the TIGER teacher evaluation system.
• At the whole school level, attention is paid to how new school priorities build on existing professional capacity and increase learning for all students.
• Whole school book study groups focus on current research and practice that attend to issues that complement district foci or that attend to issues not otherwise addressed.
• When new concepts and expectations for teacher practice are brought into the school, these are outlined in whole school sessions, but the work of analysis and application to practice takes place at the team level, with the support of the academic coach.

LEADERSHIP AND SYSTEMS THAT SUSTAIN EDUCATOR LEARNING

Clear and high expectations for professional learning.
The heat, in part, provides a set of high professional learning expectations. Everyone will:

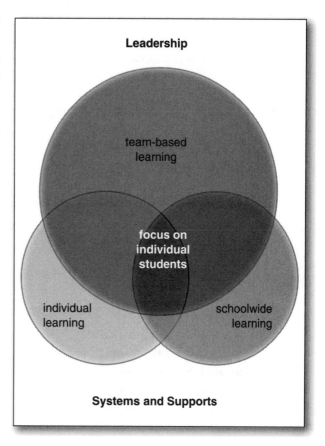

- Do everything possible to help students meet high outcomes, grow to their personal best, and meet schoolwide goals;
- Attend to personal learning goals that are based on foundational knowledge, experience, and interests, and tied to student and school goals;
- Collaborate and be flexible with colleagues in and beyond grade teams; and
- Use data to continuously track progress, and guide adjustments and changes.

Mrs. Donaldson and Mrs. King use these expectations to shape professional learning practices and resources: time, people, and materials. And these expectations frame ongoing feedback as well as formal supervision.

Differentiated professional learning that meets the needs of all adult learners. As teachers seek to support individual student needs, they work on specific content knowledge that will help students advance, think through what combinations of strategies will work for a particular learner, and, like Social Stories, what will help particular students understand themselves. This begs for professional learning that is more personalized to meet individual teacher needs and necessitates a shift from whole group learning during workshops or full-day sessions, to grade team gatherings that connect to classrooms and teaching. Differentiation for adults, as with children, requires understanding each learner's zone of proximal development: the gap between what an educator knows and can do, and her or his learning opportunities (Vygotsky, 1978). Those charged with designing professional learning are working to offer neither too little content and challenge, nor too much, but the right amount for the individual. The school culture asks educators to call upon each other and ask for support, and they do. To balance learning that arises in the moment with broader aspirations, teachers set annual, individual learning goals. For example, they recently used the Teacher Instructional Growth for Effectiveness and Results (TIGER), the evaluation model adopted by the district as part of Tennessee's efforts. To meet teachers' personal learning goals, teachers draw on professional learning resources including colleagues on grade teams, those who teach common content in other grades, and others with relevant expertise.

> **Reflection:** How is professional development personalized to meet the needs of each individual teacher in your school? What might be done to provide each educator with just-in-time support to better support unique learning goals?

Prescriptive professional learning takes place when expectations are not met. New teachers are not expected to have all the capacity they need, so the academic coach is automatically part of their professional development plan. While supervising them, the principal offers additional recommendations and ensures that supports are in place. In the case of individual teachers who are underperforming, prescription is also in order. While a teacher can be released as a last resort, there is a positive presupposition that they can meet agreed-upon expectations they have "not yet" achieved. This aligns naturally with research on effective supervision, which advocates increased scaffolded and directed learning aligning with teacher knowledge and capacity (see Danielson, 2006; Darling-Hammond, Wei et al., 2009; Glickman, Gordon, & Ross-Gordon, 2009).

District and school together tapping the right resources at the right time, and fully implementing and integrating professional learning. The district plays an important role in Tusculum View's access to professional learning, and in its capacity to integrate professional learning initiatives. For example, academic, literacy, and data coaches from Greeneville District have traveled to Atlanta to immerse themselves in formative assessment and learn how to embed it in the life of schools. Across disciplines, the coaches developed a common language and practice around formative assessment aligned with specific content, curriculum, and resources that are already in place in schools. They integrate the new learning and skills, and translate them into daily coaching practices over the course of the year. In addition, the coaches participate in their own, ongoing professional learning at the district level where they share experiences of implementing formative assessment, and how this strategy dovetails with other reforms. Kay Burke, who was the lead presenter in Atlanta, and whose materials are supporting the local work, was subsequently invited to Greeneville and numerous Tusculum View teachers are slated to attend a session with her. Coaches will have a chance to go even deeper. And the district has made sure coaches come together regularly with a master coach to build broader coaching capacity: first to learn the fundamentals of change and coaching strategies, and then to have a learning community where colleagues can support one another in trying out strategies, and then reflecting on their results.

This approach to just-in-time, integrated professional learning starts with ideas and skills for innovators who can spread the word. As more people are ready to hear the message, they introduce the source, and continue to support on-the-ground expertise to help the work solidify over time. Coaches are key resources to carry and instill innovations. Teachers at Tusculum View spoke repeatedly about coaches being able to help them make meaning of reforms and resources. There is work at the school and district level to make sure leaders have the right information needed to integrate reforms, and there is time to articulate how the different reforms and resources fit together.

This is not just the district shaping the work of schools. While district leaders vet and invest in resources based on their knowledge and understanding of overall district needs, Mrs. Donaldson and Mrs. King regularly seek resources to leverage current needs or attend to gaps in capacity, and they bring those resources to the district's attention. The school-based leaders also discern how to introduce, integrate, and leverage new initiatives in order to advance existing efforts. And they also think about the pacing of educator learning, so that the daily supports are just enough, just in time. The leaders recognize and understand that individual and collective learning happen simultaneously, and that they as leaders are important stewards of that process.

Reflection: How are reforms in your school integrated and aligned with existing schoolwide practices? What is the process for teachers to "make meaning" of new initiatives and to align them to existing knowledge and skills?

Systems for cultivating teacher and student excitement for learning.
Students and educators are free to work on their own or in groups and to
have choices wherever possible. This setting allows for many educators to
come up with ideas within the context of school and district goals, and it
allows teachers to catalyze movements within and beyond a team, such as
the example of Social Stories (see Figure 5.6).

There were numerous examples of teachers tracking resources to
engage students, manage their behavior, personalize learning strategies, and integrate technology. Staff members organize their time to
support teacher creativity, and generating ideas and supporting their
implementation is an expected part of team time. These efforts are not
an interruption of teamwork. They lie at its heart.

Figure 5.6 Video-Based Social Stories

Angie Shelton's Social Stories are three- to five-minute video narratives that
depict positive student behaviors that individual students struggle with. They
are developed as a teacher raises a behavioral concern regarding a specific
student and are designed to feature that student behaving well in what can be
a challenging situation for him or her. A video may capture a student naturally
behaving well in a particular situation. If that's not possible, they can be scripted
and students can act out how good behavior or interactions look. And they can
capture classmates describing how they work to regulate their feelings and
behaviors in a challenging situation.

How and When They Are Used at Tusculum View

When a student is struggling with a particular behavior, a teacher can suggest
that the student go and watch the video made specifically and exclusively for
that student. This allows students a break from the situation and helps them
reflect and remember how to behave. The video exists on the computer hard
drive. When other students know about the video, they may ask for their own
video: "I need help when I get angry, too." And parents may ask to have a copy
of the video to use at home.

Origins

These video stories are based on the concept of Social Stories, personalized
childhood books that illustrate and describe specific, good behaviors. The
Social Story books are a strategy of the Make a Difference project based at
Eastern Tennessee State University's Center of Excellence in Early Childhood
Learning and Development.

Source: ERIC article on Make a Difference Project: http://www.eric.ed.gov/
ERICWebPortal/search/detailmini.jsp?_nfpb=true&_&ERICExtSearch_Search
Value_0=EJ581665&ERICExtSearch_SearchType_0=no&accno=EJ581665

Figure 5.7 First-Grade Teacher Professional Development Goal

Based on your student data and your self-assessment, what is an area of knowledge or skill that you would like to strengthen? I would like to build and strengthen my knowledge of formative assessment and gain more understanding of how to use the information gained to drive my instruction. I want to look at the Common Core standards and use technology as a larger piece of formative assessment and student self-assessments.

What would success in this area look like? How will you know when you have achieved it? What would count as evidence of success? My instruction will be more tightly aligned to data from assessments given in class. I will be collaborating regularly with my team and academic coach to make my decisions for my students based on the data. I will also be giving regular, specific feeedback to my students, which will help them to have a better understanding of expectations and what success looks like. Through the use of technology, students will have a permanent portfolio of their work to see and measure progress. An increase of student achievement on formative and standardized tests will confirm success.

Figure 5.7 offers an excerpt from the individual, professional development plan of a teacher who recognizes formative assessment as a district and school priority, and who experiences the freedom to work on that priority while building on her passion for technology. Her first-grade team works collaboratively on lesson planning and design of instructional strategies, so she names them in her plan. She also mentions Mrs. Fay, a past collaborator around instructional technology issues, and the academic coach. Collaboration is initially offered to the person who initiated the idea. And if the initiative follows the school's precedent for scaling up innovations, student portfolios on flash drives or on the Cloud will spread quickly from one classroom to others.

Recreating the systems when they don't work. Mrs. Donaldson and Mrs. King describe a respectful and fundamental example of a shake-up when the school math scores were anticipated to go down. There was an external audit of instructional time, staff capacities, extra student supports, and professional learning in math. This is an example of a range of practices and systems being rethought simultaneously to close achievement gaps. As far as professional learning, teachers are expected to use the findings to differentiate instruction in mathematics, and use manipulatives and center-based learning tools. This work aligns well with their existing context, but also presses teachers to explore new ways of thinking about and planning for math instruction. The academic coach worked with teachers regularly, having a presence several days a week, and all teachers were expected to apply what they learned in professional development and coaching sessions. Whole faculty professional learning addressed data that was tracked to examine changes over time, and parent volunteers were tapped to help create math manipulatives and provide extra support in classrooms. In discussing the schoolwide initiative, teachers reported a particularly high level of value to the information and resources they learned about in workshops and coaching sessions. Implementation was scaffolded well. Together, this heat and light—with a combination of high and clear expectations, work on content and instruction, focus on data and use of resources, and support and accountability to individuals and teams—make for a set of systems that together could create a shift in student and teacher performance.

Part II

Professional Learning to Advance Equity

Findings and Practices

Equity and Supporting Core Values

6

> I have been pretty vocal about attitudes, what we can change, what we can control. We are not expecting less of X if his mother did not give him breakfast. . . . If things are difficult at home, then we are going to provide him with the best seven hours of his day.
>
> We did a book study . . . on Jensen's book, Teaching With Poverty in Mind: What Being Poor Does to Kids' Brains and What Schools Can Do About It *[2009]—and* talked about that. I require new teachers to read it. That's helped us understand a little bit about our community. Rather than allowing us to feel defeated by the number of students who come from generations of poverty, the book reaffirmed our school's culture of high expectations for all students and our use of best practices that engage, challenge, and provide avenues for academic success. What we learned from Jensen has encouraged our teachers to make more home visits and to be very intentional in planning activities to engage and partner with families. Our school's Parent Resource Center, clothes closet, parent-to-parent mentor program . . . are all outcomes of conversations from the book study.
>
> We have [also] done things where we have actually been out in our community. . . . We are . . . taking some of our parenting classes into neighborhoods and try to connect with families and offer supports to them.
>
> —Pat Donaldson, Principal,
> Tusculum View Elementary

Like Tusculum View, all the featured schools are improving student performance across the board because equity commitments shape professional learning that supports student learning. These schools are the

Advance Team for thousands of other school communities that have set high goals, committed to equity, and put the basic structures of effective schools into place. Professional learning shapes, and is shaped by, equity commitments and supporting core values.[1]

Advancing Equity With Professional Learning

Equity and Supporting Values
Focus and drive daily practices

Personalized Learning for Educators
Facilitates individual student success

Leadership and Systems
Sustain and guide continuous improvement

The first chapter laid out three school characteristics that advance equity (see box). Chapters 6, 7, and 8 explore these characteristics in relation to findings. Chapter 6 focuses on equity issues, Chapter 7 takes up personalizing student learning, and Chapter 8 examines systems and leadership methods. The professional learning practices discussed in the following sections were prominent in at least three of the four schools, unless otherwise noted.

*   *   *

EQUITY AND SUPPORTING CORE VALUES

Finding

Equity is the fundamental value, visible through public commitments and specific practices. Supporting values—continuous learning for all, collaboration, and collective responsibility for everyone learning—further enliven equity at each school. These values together are non-negotiable drivers of improvement.

Interviews, review of materials, and school visits quickly affirmed schools' commitment to equity and justice is clear, public, and evident in multiple ways across the school. Three supporting practices emerged:

1. Continuous learning and improvement for every student and educator

2. Collaboration

3. Collective responsibility for everyone learning

These are not *pro forma* or aspirational values. Together they are drivers at the schools. They are ways of being. They shape how people make decisions, the decisions they make, and their behavior. Together, the values and related practices across the schools reveal their culture.[2] Educators both name and act on these values. They also revisit them and seek ongoing relevance and consistency, recognizing that "a measure of the strength of a school's espoused values is in the faculty's willingness to challenge the expression of contradictory values in words or practice."[3]

Equity Explicit

Equity is the fundamental value at each school. Educators communicate that every student deserves to be understood and to

> **Plain Talk About Equity Commitments**
>
> Here are some ways featured schools articulated their commitment to every student doing well:
>
> - Students will score at least 80% on key assessments (whatever the proficiency score is), or get support until they do.
> - Meeting the needs of *all* students is not "extra" work . . . it is *the* work.
> - Every student will graduate ready for college.
> - Every student will make *at least* one year's progress.
> - Every student and teacher will achieve their personal best.
> - We don't just conference with the "problem" students. We conference with *all* the students.
> - Our vision is to achieve social justice through the development of the complete individual.

learn at very high standards. It is explicit in mission, vision, value documents, communications with the community, and explanations of programs. At Montgomery, if students don't achieve proficiency on key assignments, more time is spent on task, a lesson is retaught, and/or additional supports are provided until the goal is met. Robust strategies to reframe and revisit instruction demonstrate that the commitment to equity is serious. Only systematic follow-through achieves equity and excellence as ultimate goals (McKenzie et al., 2008; Scheurich & Skrla, 2003; Shields, 2003).

Equity visible in professional learning. Educators at all schools note that equity is directly addressed in different ways (see Table 6.1). All educators consider using data as central to equity work, as is differentiating instruction. At the same time, schools named activities not typically considered professional learning as key ways to support understanding about equity.

Discussion as professional learning on equity. Formal and informal conversations deepen understanding and expectations of equity.

Table 6.1   Examples of Professional Learning Topics Related to Working on Equity

All schools:

- Use the data to inform what the student performance is, and use high expectations to shape instruction and supports
- Differentiate learning to honor different interests, intelligences, and capacities
- Name and discuss specific expectations, and how they will be manifested and tracked
- Confront expressions of low expectations regarding a particular child or a group of children
- Use shared readings as a way to build common understanding about equity

One or more schools:

- Work collectively to understand general issues of race, class, language and culture, privilege—cultural competency
- Explore personal bias, how it impedes student learning, school and district practices, and what to do about it
- Design antiracist, antibias curriculum and assessments
- Use instructional materials that acknowledge and incorporate the backgrounds of students
- Participate in a simulation where participants take on the role of economically poor people in different circumstances
- Consider different dimensions of learners by developing interest inventories, learn about multiple intelligences, use True Colors or Myers-Briggs Inventory
- Learn about family strengths and contexts, their structures, values, and patterns
- Conduct student home visits
- Use student survey data to ensure students feel personally supported in their learning

Leaders select and expect staff to read and discuss specific equity-related texts (Yang, 2009). Equity arises in conversations about climate and expectations. When one teacher said, "That kid will never . . . ," the leader responded, "We're not going to talk like that. I want you to talk about each kid as if it is your kid. We're going to give every kid everything we have got. We are going to treat every child like they are our child." In the context of an almost exclusive Caucasian student body, that conversation is about equity regarding economic class and some special needs. Leaders don't tolerate biased conversations or practices that lower expectations. "Since those belief systems exist outside the school, you create a wall of protection . . . you don't let that spill into the [school] culture."

The Social Justice Humanitas Academy's name announces what's at its center. Its faculty regularly discusses race, class, culture, gender, and power as a regular part of their professional learning. Reflection happens individually and as a community. Educators become prepared to facilitate these challenging conversations with students as they relate to the curriculum, to advisory topics, and to life in general. Educators at SJ Humanitas value cultural competence for teachers and for students as they go out into the world, who are often breaking from family tradition by going to college. Students are prepared personally and academically to succeed in programs and professions that have not historically included them.

Professional Learning: Understanding Students as Persons

Focus on equity begins with understanding students as individuals. This information is important to everyone working with students. What are their backgrounds? What are their perceptions and interests? What supports do they have at home? Schools actively build relationships, inventories of interests, and understand multiple intelligences on an ongoing basis.

Equity, collaboration, continuous learning, and collective responsibility entwined. *Here are some ways schools expressed the interconnection of these values:*

"Stults Road thrives on student achievement. Our commitment to professional learning communities helps to develop independent, critical-thinking, goal-oriented learners." (School website, description of general program)

"As a faculty member of Social Justice Humanitas Academy (SJHA), I understand I am asked to put students' needs first at all times. When planning the curriculum, I agree to work creatively to meet the diverse learning styles and needs of our student population. I have read and agree with the SJHA mission statement and intend to use project-based, constructive learning whenever possible in my curriculum. In order to do this, I agree to teach, plan, and reflect collaboratively" (Social Justice Humanitas Academy Elect-to-Work Agreement, 2011–2012).

"Offering each of our students the highest quality education possible requires that our parents, teachers, and other members of our community combine efforts. Effective communication among these partners will enable us to maintain and strengthen a strong well-rounded educational program for each student. Educating our children to live in an increasingly complex society demands the very best efforts of all of us who have a vested interest in education at Tusculum View" (School statement of mission and philosophy).

Family engagement as professional learning that advances equity. All four schools engage with families and the community as part of professional learning. An understanding of family structures and communities, where and how students live, and their heritage all help teachers understand and embrace students for who they are. For one school, that means making home visits to families.

Three schools offer classes to families. One school helped several parents learn enough to join the school staff. This school's science scores have outpaced the state's in part because family members are engaged early and often to understand science projects and to work on them concretely with children.

Values that enable equity: continuous learning, collaboration, and collective responsibility. Though not automatically equated with equity, these three values are central in equity and school identity conversations. They enable an equity commitment to take hold.

Continuous learning and improvement for every student and educator. Equity requires that all students learn, think about their learning, and get extra supports when they exceed or fall short of expectations. Educators need similar learning experiences as they set goals, try new practices, and reflect on their progress. Tim Knipe, award-winning teacher leader and founding teacher of Social Justice Humanitas Academy, described it this way:

> I found that the more I tried, [the more] I was learning something that kept me going . . . it was such a charge. . . . It's like jumping out of an airplane. The first time you do it they attach you to a ripcord because you black out. You jump out of the airplane but you never think about opening your parachute. You just go into shock. Teaching is a little bit like that. You do it the first time; you're in shock. It takes a while to figure out where the ripcord is, how to pull the right levers. As I started to become more cognizant, I sought out the people who really knew what they were doing; they all belonged to this group, the Humanitas group. I would observe them. They would come and observe me and say, "What about this?"

At these schools, iterative professional learning is as fundamental to equity as student learning. There is space and honor for the intricacies of the teaching craft and schoolwide reform, for making mistakes, and for continued problem solving and learning leading to excellence. Continued improvement approaches deepen learning, and remaining achievement gaps and glitches are tracked doggedly. As one principal summarized, "We are never satisfied."

Collaboration. In the schools studied, collaboration is neither a nicety nor a choice. No one person knows everything, all the time, about how to help each student. Professional communities facilitate exploring questions of practice, brainstorming great ideas, tapping resources, understanding data, and applying findings. An instructional conundrum, a student's need for support beyond what the teacher can provide, or a teacher coming new to the school or the profession can all catalyze collaboration.

Relational trust and care facilitate effective collaboration (Bryk & Schneider, 2002). José Navarro, at SJ Humanitas, goes to great lengths to continually remind teachers and students that they are persons worthy of offering and receiving compassion, before anything else.[4,5] He offers Weekly Challenges to encourage caring across the community, and deepens compassion as part of professional learning. Each school deliberately encourages and expresses care, supporting collaboration both initially and when times are tough.

Collaboration can be challenging, as teachers noted. "They have to deal with people who are a pain in the ass." There can be exceptions in the goal to work with everyone: "I can ask *almost* anyone for help." But in each school, collaboration is a source of professional productivity, nourishment, even joy. Teachers repeatedly said, "I love my team. I can't live without them" or "I don't know what I would have done without . . ."

Collective responsibility: everyone is responsible for all the children and for the school doing well. Collaboration starts with joint task processes. Each school has an expectation that teachers claim responsibility for more than "their" students. A Stults Road leader said that collective responsibility is built into the school day and schedule. One administrator said, "Targeted instruction time exists for everyone [in the building]. We always rotate the kids; we [administrators] support every teacher to work with every level. . . . Each student has to know multiple teachers, so that gives them a lot of people who care about their learning." This responsibility and persistence extends to students, who are expected to take charge of their learning, understand their own progress and the next steps against a goal, and then to family members' support of learning.

*   *   *

The next two chapters look at practices of professional learning in an equity context, with analysis of the supports in place to frame the work at every step.

Reflection: What might be keeping people at your school from getting to productive conversations about equity?

Who in your school has permission to raise concerns about practice when equity goals are not met? Is this responsibility shared widely, or permitted among only a few leaders? What specific changes might enable the majority of teachers to become comfortable enough to name and resolve issues of practice?

Is working with parents to learn about and support students done systematically, or is it up to individual teacher discretion? What specific efforts could extend the capacity of educators to support students through family engagement?

How do you build collective responsibility in your school, so that educators talk more about "our students" than "my students"? What indicators show that teachers and leaders have a sense of responsibility for equity outcomes?

Source: Stults Road website (http://www.edline.net/pages/Stults_Road_Elementary/Pages/Our_Program). Retrieved December 14, 2012.

NOTES

1.   Rather than "values," Hirsh and Killion (2009) discuss seven principles of professional learning, which have overlap with findings in this chapter, as well as Chapters 7 and 8.

2.   A definition of school culture includes "deep patterns of values, beliefs, and traditions that have been formed" (Deal & Peterson, 1990).

3.   Written communications with Nancy Love, October 2012.

4.   Research on relational trust has demonstrated that schools with high levels of relational trust are more likely to improve (Barth, 2001; Bryk & Schneider, 2002; Hoy & Tschannen-Moran, 2003).

5.   Hargreaves and Fullan (2012) refer to this as social capital, "how the quantity and quality of interactions and social relationships among people affects their access to knowledge and information; their senses of expectations, obligation, and trust; and how far they are likely to adhere to the same norms or codes of behavior" (pp. 88–92).

Personalized Adult and Student Learning 7

"It was a PD pinnacle," Principal Navarro recounts.

Together the special education teacher and principal had created an Individual Pupil Education Plan (IPEP, see page 58), for each student. The principal made a spreadsheet to organize a range of data points that frame the IPEP. "We wanted to look at grades, English Language Learning test scores, reflections on 40 Developmental Assets for Adolescents, and other assessment results," Mr. Navarro said. This was a Data Day. "Data Days are PD days dedicated to data analysis and the creation of lessons and action plans based on that data. Every five weeks, the week after grades are due, we get together as a whole school and as grade-level teams and look at all of our students through the lens of multiple data points." For the first time, teachers added to the spreadsheets by mapping on students' dominant, multiple intelligences (MI). Teachers administer MI inventories to get to know their students, and then use them in grade team discussions about individual students and to plan instruction. Each lesson at SJ Humanitas aims to teach to at least four intelligences. In their analysis, a trend surfaced: 40% of the lowest-performing students were bodily-kinesthetic learners. Teachers in teams immediately start considering relevant instructional strategies.

"We never had all that data in one place at one time before. This took years for teachers to develop a way to [collect and organize the data and] look at all of them systematically. . . . It was a matter of everything lining up, getting through the mandated PD days to have the time to focus on students. What has taken so long is finding a whole school that . . . is collecting our students' data and using it to inform our policies as an institutional value. "We use our advisory lessons as a way to collect data, teachers have been given conference periods to desegregate and analyze data, and then as a school we analyze the data during 'data days.'

"We're working to address each student's individual needs through interdisciplinary curriculum, go deep in content with strategies based on how our students actually learn—putting all this into an individualized frame for student learning," says Mr. Navarro. "As individuals, we may not know how to respond to it. But as a team . . ."

**Advancing Equity With
Professional Learning**

Equity and Supporting Values
Focus and drive daily practices

Personalized Learning for Educators
Facilitates individual student success

Leadership and Systems
Sustain and guide continuous improvement

This account points to the many aligned and complementary steps and data points Social Justice Humanitas Academy engages to help teachers support individual students. This chapter explores the common personalizing practices for student and professional learning across schools. In the featured schools, teachers, administrators, and other staff focus their energies on each student's learning, sometimes catching up to meet standards, sometimes going beyond them as they are met. Like their students, educators learn continuously. To make classroom learning engaging, challenging, and personalized, educators synchronize their efforts with colleagues. As personalized instruction skills become more precise, educator questions about practice become more pointed. School-based professional learning must then keep up with these new demands at the individual, team, and schoolwide levels.

Finding

Focus on equity compels educators to become increasingly precise in personalizing student learning, which then presses for alignment among individual, team, and whole school learning. It shifts professional learning content, processes, and contexts in fundamental ways. Teachers become motivated to use ongoing, formative assessment practices to understand students' individual learning needs.

The scope and momentum of adult learning is framed by clear, persistent, and high expectations for every student, regardless of background, race, culture, economic class, language, gender, or ability. Personalized student learning is required to meet these expectations, within and beyond the classroom. Educators experience pride in their craft, a sense of efficacy, and a desire to keep doing better. Successes are not the result of compliance with hard-hitting external accountability; they are internally driven by ambitious goals and supports to facilitate achievement that exceeds regulatory requirements.

PERSONALIZED STUDENT LEARNING THAT FOCUSES PROFESSIONAL LEARNING

Featured schools employ documented practices to improve achievement, within and beyond class time. And then they push further, to ensure that each student is advancing. These methods become the focus of professional learning.

Common Focus on the Instructional Core

Chapter 1 postulated that featured schools would focus on the instructional core to narrow achievement gaps and synchronize rigorous content, effective pedagogical practices, and assessment practices. Interviews, student and teacher artifacts, and success on indicators confirmed this assumption. In this sense, there were no surprises in visiting the schools. But it was extraordinary to find the level of comprehensive systems, frequency and precision in understanding students' gifts and needs, and the focus on support for each student's moving to the next level.

School leaders work to ensure that the content is highly challenging and that teachers have or can easily access curriculum content appropriate to each student's learning level. These schools are well ahead of others applying the Common Core standards. Social Justice Humanitas measures rigor against college entry exams and the University of California freshman curriculum.

Strategies for Ensuring Deep Implementation

- Student strengths and needs are at the center of agenda items and conversations
- Consistent, scheduled meeting time, at least weekly
- Preparation and effective facilitation of meetings
- Clarity and role definition for team leaders and members
- Schoolwide use of protocols for discussion, decision making, and feedback
- Close monitoring of team practices
- Support for team leaders
- Continuity of leadership
- Scheduled opportunities to share practices across teams

Teachers have a range of instructional strategies at the ready to engage students, and will often apply multiple strategies simultaneously to meet varied instructional needs. Tusculum View, in its fourth year of implementing Tomlinson's differentiated instruction model, demonstrates a wide and deep repertoire of instructional practices. While every school does not reference Tomlinson, they all share her understanding about content and pedagogy. Differentiation is a way of thinking about what students need, and shows how to draw from varied strategies, based on specific, individual student needs, not just adding instructional moves and programs haphazardly.[1]

Use of Evidence to Personalize Instruction

The schools have facility with data and its meaning. Summative and benchmark assessment tools demonstrate general trends, and formative assessment practices and short-term data cycles come to the center, to provide precise understanding about students and instruction. Each school's data use approximately follows Love, Stiles, Mundry, and DiRanna's (2008) Data Pyramid (see Figure 7.1).

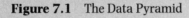

Figure 7.1 The Data Pyramid

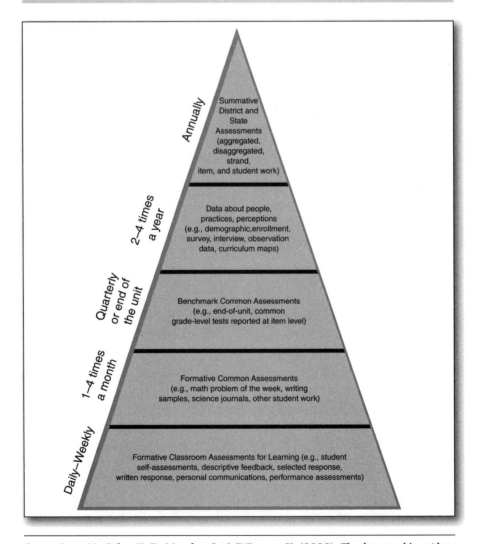

Source: Love, N., Stiles, K. E., Mundry, S., & DiRanna, K. (2008). *The data coach's guide to improving learning for all students: Unleashing the power of collaborative inquiry* (p. 129, Figure 4.1). Thousand Oaks, CA: Corwin. Reprinted with permission.

Educators have made the leap from simply using routine data analysis processes, to using the findings to make changes in instruction, instructional time, and extra supports. Tusculum View, for example, is implementing classroom formative assessment. Each grade is conducting nine-week systematic data cycles, and teachers are using that data to guide pre-assessments and weekly progress reflection sheets, to gain understanding of mastery and "not yet." Each school has a Response to Intervention (RTI) model, all teachers look at data, and they invite staff with specialized expertise for support when needed. Data-use practices are highlighted in the box below. And it is not just adults who are looking at evidence: Students are also taking responsibility for their own progress by setting learning

> **Using Evidence to Personalize Learning**
>
> All schools engaged in these practices
>
> - Conduct short-term data review cycles within a team context
> - Use formative assessment evidence, alongside benchmark and other data
> - Apply data analysis findings to practice immediately
> - Administer benchmark assessments in five- to nine-week cycles
> - Review data in teams and determine together how to help each student
> - Conference with students to look at data and consider what's next for their learning
> - Include attendance and tardiness logs, scores on assignments, and benchmark data results in data reviews
> - Dovetail the Response to Intervention model with the data review process
> - Survey students about their learning interests, practices, and experiences, and use the data to inform practice

goals, reviewing their progress, and thinking about future learning. When work is not up to par, they go back and redo, until it is.

PROFESSIONAL LEARNING THAT SUPPORTS ENGAGING STUDENTS AS PERSONS AND LEARNERS

The first chapter proposed that educators in schools that personalized instruction and high performance would have solid, ongoing, job-embedded professional learning. While many schools work on the nuts and bolts of professional learning, they don't often make the progress found at the four featured schools. Table 7.1 shows professional learning practices present in at least three of the schools, organized by individual, team, and whole school approaches.

These practices are in evidence at the schools, though no one claims to have perfected the formula. Each community continues to grapple with the next, best practice given their circumstances and goals.

Table 7.1 Individual, Team, and Whole School Learning Practices Across Sites

Individual Learning	Team Learning
Individual Learning Goals	*Grade-Level/Multigrade Teams*
Teachers set goals based on schoolwide priorities, student learning data, and individual needs and gifts. The principal, coach, and sometimes colleagues know these goals, which frame professional dialogue. Teachers collect and share evidence on progress.	Each teacher has a primary go-to team. Based on timely student data, meetings provide structure for learning, instruction planning, strategy sharing, assessment, and personalizing instruction.
Coaching and Modeling	*Vertical Teams*
Teachers approach colleagues as sources of best practice and to get feedback on their work. Schools with coaches have more intensive and structured programs, yet each site provides teachers with direct feedback.	Complementing grade teams, vertical teams align standards across grades. To personalize instruction, teachers learn about standards at other grade levels, and how to help trailing, succeeding, and excelling students.
Peer Observations	*Team Leadership*
Educators learn using a structured peer observation process, with protocols and clear expectations. The culture of observation includes informal visits to other classrooms to observe a lesson and offer feedback or learn a new practice.	Team leaders may be members who receive support as a leader, a coach, or principal. They guide process, align priorities, and deepen practice over time.
Self-Initiated Learning	*Data Team*
Each site encourages self-initiated learning, which is shared and cultivated through team and whole school forums, building capacity, and integrating individual interests with school priorities.	Three schools have a data team that tracks on benchmark and interim assessment results. They regularly report back to teams and individuals on progress, and activate teacher supports when needed.
	Scheduled Team Time
	Teams have structured meeting times to focus on and complete curriculum, instruction, and assessment tasks. Minimum meeting time is one hour per week, and in all schools, teams held additional meetings.

Whole School Learning

Attending to the big picture: Leaders propose and frame priorities. Educators make meaning, develop shared understanding, and collectively clarify key messages.

Reflection as integral to practice: Communities make time for reflection to build shared understanding and professional capacity, and to assure sustained implementation.

Knowing each other as persons and learners: Gatherings promote relational trust and support. Reflective dialogue practices and protocols encourage shared beliefs and experiences.

Shared accountability: Progress is celebrated. Teacher/team learning goals are public and reviewed. Lack of progress stimulates new strategies to ensure success.

Professional learning content, process, and context. At the individual, team, and whole school level, there is a need for solid professional learning, appropriate processes, and supportive contexts. Professional learning content, process, and context are described in Figures 7.2, 7.3, and 7.4, respectively. The left-hand column of each figure specifies a typical school's practices. The right-hand column names practices found in at least three of the featured schools. The schools have developed them to the point where they have solid structures and practices in multiple areas. They are moving, or have moved, to professional practices that personalize student learning and systematically advance equity. Content, process, and context are fundamental to professional learning, and are a foundation for national professional learning standards (Mizell, Hord, Killion, & Hirsh, 2011).

Content of professional learning. Professional learning encompasses knowledge and skills about both subject areas and pedagogy, and using evidence to inform learning. It also includes climate and community, change management, and learning.

Content mastery is valued. The principals at both Montgomery and Tusculum View said that new math strategies and content needed to be high quality, while teachers needed substantive working knowledge of application. Surface knowledge or knowledge of their own grade's standards are not enough. Leaders' deep knowledge of math content and strategies contribute to the degree that they help teachers meet individual needs.

Case schools used book studies to shape consistent understanding of key content in equity, instruction, and assessment. Following book studies, educators held themselves accountable for providing feedback on implementation of new techniques and tools. Selected books were also included in new teacher orientation, to build consistent expectations amongst incoming faculty.

Professional learning processes. Processes "integrate theories, research, and models of human learning to achieve . . . intended outcomes" (Learning Forward, 2011). Educator designs attend to learning needs. Though these are mostly team processes, the overall design also attends to individual and schoolwide learning (see Chapter 8). Beth O'Brien, at Montgomery, engaged Critical Friends protocols and professional learning community frameworks to set the stage for whole school professional dialogue, and then led an introduction to PLC development. Simultaneously, she worked extensively on processes for organizing assessments and data to clarify student progress and needs.

Figure 7.2 Content of Professional Learning to Advance Equity and Personalization

Content of professional learning in many schools		Content of professional learning in schools focused on equity and personalization
Educators develop deep knowledge of content and learning outcomes aligned to grade-level expectations.		Educators collectively develop deep knowledge of content that includes an understanding of how learning develops over time, and establish learning outcomes that transcend specific grade-level expectations.
Teams use data to understand performance trends and improve their planning focus for instruction.		Teams analyze a range of data, and explore evidence of student learning to plan the next steps in instruction for each student.
Teams collectively develop skills to employ a range of instructional strategies, and know when it is appropriate to use them.		Teachers collectively hone their capacity to draw on a range of instructional strategies to better support specific students in meeting differentiated learning outcomes.
Educators learn about students as persons and learners at the start of the year, probe more about some students throughout the year, and episodically learn about others.		Educators together develop strategies to continually understand the strengths and needs of each learner, through practices including conferring, use of student tracking tools, and portfolios.
Educators learn about equity as aspiration and have some goals for narrowing achievement gaps.		Educators collectively clarify and agree to systematic equity expectations, and engage in understanding their own biases, their students, and family contexts.

Professional learning context. Chapter 1 suggested that professional learning would apply to three contexts—individual, team, and whole school—with all of them having a focus on individual student learning. This proved correct across the four schools.

Figure 7.3   Professional Learning Processes to Advance Equity and Personalization

Professional learning processes in some schools		Professional learning processes in schools focused on equity and personalization
Professional learning processes are organized to expose everyone to basic concepts and skills connected to school goals.		Professional learning processes are personalized and adapted to reflect the learning goals of teachers and teams.
Teachers set annual professional learning goals aligned with schoolwide initiatives and goals, and report to the principal on their progress in meeting individual learning goals.		Teachers set annual professional learning goals and hold each other accountable for meeting individual learning goals in team and/or whole school settings.
Professional learning takes place at the individual, team, and whole school levels, but learning in each setting is not consistently aligned to the other settings or to educator needs.		Individual, team, and whole school learning is aligned and coherent, and each learning environment has a specific role in developing individual knowledge and skills for sustained, schoolwide implementation.
Some effective resources and adult learning strategies are applied to different professional learning forums.		A wide range of resources and differentiated learning are applied for individual educators, based on school goals and individual learning needs.

Individual teacher learning requires more than *pro forma* completion of professional learning plans. Each teacher is responsible for personal improvement, regularly tracks their strengths and needs, and then reaches out to those within and beyond the community who can help.

Team learning is the central forum for professional learning. There is one team that is home base for each teacher: the first place to bring problems, to share understanding of children, to troubleshoot, to be safe. At three schools, this is the grade-level team. As a small school, Montgomery has multigrade primary, elementary, and middle school teams. It is on these teams that teachers practice thinking about and taking responsibility for students, whether or not they were teaching them at that time. Teachers learn about all the students for whom they are collectively, as a team, responsible. This extends to content-based

Figure 7.4 Professional Learning Contexts to Advance Equity and Personalization

Professional learning contexts in many schools		Professional learning contexts in schools focused on equity and personalization
Professional learning takes place within the individual, team, and whole school contexts; learning in each area is not necessarily aligned or coherent.		Professional learning takes place "continuously" during formally scheduled times, and at varied times throughout the day. Teachers plan impromptu meetings based on emerging or pressing student needs.
The majority of professional learning time is spent developing teacher skills and knowledge.		The majority of professional learning time supports teachers to identify student learning needs and explore how to best to address instructional next steps for each student.
Team meetings allow teachers with common students to meet; these are scheduled a minimum of once weekly.		Leaders use a wide range of strategies to extend team time to multiple opportunities weekly.
Whole school professional development takes place within allocated (district-determined) blocks of time.		Whole school professional learning often extends beyond district expectations to ensure regular, aptly timed meetings for teachers to address schoolwide learning.
Time is allocated primarily for introduction and early implementation of new skills and knowledge.		Time required to learn, implement, and sustain practice is planned for when new initiatives are introduced. Leaders aim to provide sufficient time for content mastery and full implementation.
There is a wide disparity of educator interest and engagement in learning and skill building.		All educators are highly engaged in the learning process and skill building.
External content experts often plan and lead school-based professional learning.		School-based educators actively plan and lead school-based professional learning.

teams attending to alignment and resources, or student support, or convened to address a particular issue.

The whole school sessions are a time for big ideas, reflection on or grappling with practice, lack of alignments, "struggle in the service of integration," celebration, or some combination.

Individual, team, and whole school learning each have a distinct charge. There is intentionality and precision about educator improvement and directly addressing student needs. Evidence determines needs, the right expertise is tapped, and adults learn to apply new concepts and skills.

Time, the *sine qua non* of any professional learning context, cannot be taken for granted in this discussion. Across schools the provision of time, time management, and facilitating use of that time to focus on individual learning needs receives continual attention and reframing. There is also recognition that personalizing learning leads to colleagues frequently tapping each other, and three of the schools built common planning periods into their daily schedules, so teacher dialogue could take place when needed, beyond formal team meeting time.

ADVANCING PROFESSIONAL LEARNING
THAT SUPPORTS EQUITY AND JUSTICE

Increasing precision in teaching and learning does not happen automatically. No teacher, even the best prepared, arrives ready to engage the panoply of human possibilities that reveal themselves in a classroom. When the charge goes beyond standard achievement by just "the best" teachers, and asks all teachers to meet the mark with all students, the professional learning is focused, multifaceted, and systemic. The next chapter looks at the systems and the leadership that sustain the work.

> **Reflection:** What steps is your school taking to add classroom-level evidence to large-scale data analysis? What might be a next step for your school to align classroom instruction more tightly with the data? What do you have to give up in order for this to happen?
>
> In your school setting, to what degree are school teams primarily led by teachers and focused on complex issues of practice? How do teams draw upon both data and professional judgment in their discussions and decision making?

NOTE

1. "Differentiation is more than a strategy or series of strategies—it is a way of thinking about teaching and learning... Practicing quality differentiation is much more about knowing what matters to teach, realizing that learning happens in us rather than to us, continually reflecting on the 'particularness' of each of our students, and pondering how to develop both the commonalities students share as humans and the singularities students bring as individuals. If we as teachers understood the nature of our art more fully and deeply, more differentiation would likely evolve from that understanding. Learning some new 'tricks' with little sense of why they matter is less helpful" (Tomlinson & Allen, 2000, p.14).

Leadership and Systems   **8**

Ms. Jaramillo at Stults Road Elementary has deep skill and a flair for differentiating. She does it in Spanish and English, while looping across grades 3 and 4. The district is providing systemic support of differentiation, offering professional learning and coaching to deepen expertise of some teachers who are already employing formative assessment practices and strategies for differentiation. The district will then expand systemwide support, in part, by helping selected teachers support colleagues at their school. All good, but the Stults Road leadership team can't wait. Leaders name the opportunity to deepen equity through differentiation practices now.

A few months into the effort, Principal Amber Leblond asks Ms. Jaramillo and other selected teachers to share the new instructional practices, and all teachers are asked to try them out. Follow-up happens the Stults Road way, with teachers working on new practices in their classrooms, getting support through team dialogue, and clarifying in whole school sessions how this new work aligns to current practice. Educators at the school level follow the district lead, but make it their own. And everyone will keep at it until they achieve mastery.

This chapter shows how leadership and systems build professional capital at all four schools, advance equity, and personalize learning. Like the Stults Road Elementary example above, all schools continuously develop professional capital: the collective knowledge, skills as individuals and collaborators, and the ability to make effective decisions together.[1]

Their work involves both leadership and systems, combined not

Advancing Equity With Professional Learning

Equity and Supporting Values
Focus and drive daily practices

Personalized Learning for Educators
Facilitates individual student success

Leadership and Systems
Sustain and guide continuous improvement

because they are synonymous, but because when we talk about professional learning, equity, and personalization, we are inevitably talking about work that goes beyond the classroom.

Each of the featured schools has developed improvement systems, with varied feedback loops and check points that leverage professional learning. The work of leadership is to guide and influence these systems—how individual and small-scale efforts relate to one another and how they contribute to equity goals. Conversely, systems without leaders render only piecemeal results.[2] See Figure 8.1 for specific systems and Figure 8.2 for leadership practices.

Finding

A clear and detailed understanding of how learning happens is applied to both the way students learn and the way educators learn, as they seek to improve their knowledge and their skills. Professional learning mirrors personalized student learning and is sustained by leadership and support systems.

PROFESSIONAL LEARNING MIRRORS PERSONALIZED STUDENT LEARNING

In each school, adult and student learning look surprisingly alike. The same conditions and supports students receive when instruction is personalized, educators receive through professional learning. Educators tap prior knowledge and connect it to new concepts, make meaning with others, reserve time for reflection, experiment with application, practice over time, and demonstrate mastery. Mistakes are valued. People who try and fail, try again[3] and build resilience.[4]

There are important parallels between student and adult learning experiences. As student teams are given rigorous challenges and scaffolded supports, so too are adult teams. As the whole class learns about big themes and outcomes, so too are teachers introduced to big ideas in schoolwide or even districtwide professional learning. Formative data upstages summative data, as it informs both next steps in student learning and current professional best practice (e.g., lesson plans, instructional materials and classroom artifacts, insights drawn from conferring with teachers, individual and team learning goals, and student assessment results).

In each of the featured schools there is a shared vision of effective learning, increasingly focused on personalized instruction, applied to both student and professional learning. As a coach said, "If we are asking teachers to do this [personalize learning] with students, then we have to do it for teachers."

For example, teachers speak of how they value practice, feedback, and refinement to meet their personalized goals, and use evidence to guide their own next steps in learning.

At three schools, educators intentionally learn in the presence of students. They give one another feedback in class, confer with one another, and try out different practices for each other. This professional learning embedded in the school day models learning for students, and provides "just in time" learning for educators. In these schools, it's likely to see a teacher seeking support or sharing with a colleague, while students are simultaneously engaged in learning.

Figure 8.1   Systems for Professional Learning That Advance Equity

Systems for professional learning in some schools		Systems for professional learning in schools focused on equity and personalization
Individual educators are encouraged to seek out opportunities for feedback and reflection, and may revise practice over time. They are not supported systemwide.		Learning is personalized for adults and students. Systems ensure continuous cycles of practice, reflection, feedback, and revision, until new learning is mastered.
Opportunities for individual, team, and whole school learning are occasionally available and sporadically integrated.		Adult learning systems ensure that educators engage with new ideas at the individual, team, and schoolwide levels. Feedback loops ensure balance and coherence between levels and across all three.
Feedback systems may de-motivate adult learning and decrease intrinsic motivation through negative feedback loops and punitive evaluation models.		The feedback systems for adult learning encourage intrinsic motivation and internal responsibility.
While there is confidence in teacher capacity to learn and innovate, teachers largely do not get feedback on their individual progress toward goals or appropriate supports to do better.		A system monitors attainment of individual, team, and whole school learning goals. Multiple feedback loops ensure that teachers are making progress in their learning, and strategies are activated if they are not.

LEADERS, NOT LEADER: THE NEED
FOR MULTIPLE AGENTS

While leadership can be synonymous with "principal," all four schools have multiple educators, both formal and/or informal, sharing in the functions of leading professional learning, practicing distributed leadership—not one leader, but "the web of leaders, followers, and their situations that gives form to leadership practice" (Spillane & Diamond, 2007). Social Justice Humanitas established distributed leadership through their pilot model, creating formal roles for two lead teachers who are responsible for designing professional learning. The Design Team takes responsibility for professional learning partnerships. In other schools, multiple leaders have evolved, through staffing changes or grant funding, creating combinations of principals, coaches, and specialists who lead professional learning.

Increasing the focus on equity requires distributed leadership. Managing and integrating the student and adult learning systems are simply too much work for one person. Diverse roles and perspectives are needed for it to work well. While the number of formal and informal leaders in each school varies, teachers are usually involved in schoolwide, professional learning issues. As this interest becomes more regular and deliberate, practices and systems become formalized.

> ### Shared Acts of Leadership in Support of Student and Professional Learning
>
> In the schools studied, many teachers participated in work that is traditionally the domain of principals or other formal leaders:
>
> - Being the main contact for an external professional learning partner
> - Visiting a colleague's classroom when a teacher is struggling with a specific practice, whether or not they have asked for help
> - Mapping out professional learning priorities and mapping out the time needed to fully implement each, and setting priorities
> - Optimizing the school schedule to maximize professional learning during the day, without forfeiting student learning
> - Visiting a teacher's classroom to learn about a new practice, and sharing what they learned with colleagues
> - Naming professional learning priorities six months in advance, based on current teacher work and student learning

Learning leaders providing support. Each educator has at least one person considering their professional learning with them. That person is responsible for being "a couple of steps ahead," as one school coach put it, in terms of knowing what each adult will need to grow, in the context of specific students' needs and school direction. Those are the *learning leaders* in the school. They have deep expertise and help build on educators' existing skills, though they don't need to be experts in every area. They are likely to follow current reform thinking and practice.

Systems of individual, team, and whole school professional learning. Successful leaders pay attention to individual, team, and whole school learning that, taken together, describe a system of professional learning. They coordinate and align the three, both two at a time, and as a whole.

OVERLAPS IN THE VENN DIAGRAM

The schools show that professional learning takes place at all three levels. They practice careful integration, and align efforts to achieve successful capacity building and continuous growth.

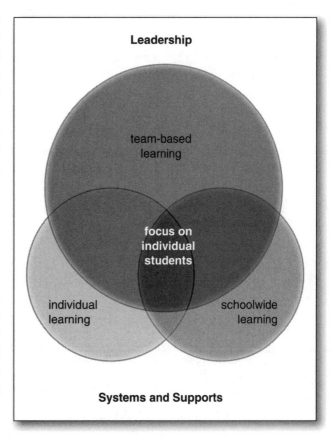

Individual and team learning overlap is primary. Individuals bring questions of practice to the team for consideration and resolution, and team discussions influence individual practice. At Tusculum View, third-grade teachers write individual, professional learning goals together with an intention of supporting one another in achieving them.

Team and whole school learning overlap as teams test general, big picture understandings. Expectations are clarified as important questions are puzzled out in the whole school context, so there is cohesion around issues that affect everyone. Teams take up big-picture issues and make specific meaning relating to their grades. Teams also bring issues to the whole school forum by sharing successful practices and raising challenges with schoolwide implications.

Whole school and individual professional learning underscores the importance of applying global initiatives to individual practice. Evaluation systems require individual learning goals that relate to goals for student achievement and the school as a whole. Individual practice can also support the whole school. For example, an experienced teacher of gifted and talented students arrived new to a school and was asked immediately upon arrival to share a specific strategy with the whole school. Learning leaders invited everyone to adapt the strategy to their circumstances, and then tracked implementation.

A coherent learning system aligns individual, team, and whole school learning. When Tusculum View, for example, aligned new elementary math standards to their existing programs, they noticed that teachers needed to learn key aspects of conceptual math. The academic coach approached this work through the lens of all three contexts—whole school, team, and individual learning—in order to introduce and deepen new math pedagogy. She led afterschool workshops with many teachers, and invited teachers from other district schools to join. She helped individual teachers and teams try out new approaches in classrooms, she showed how the new resources connected with current practice, and provided model lessons and feedback. Teams took up the charge and together explored new materials and lessons. When the district came forward the following year with a new math initiative, Tusculum View teachers were ready. Mrs. King could "take it deeper," and then teams further spread the wealth.

Tusculum View already has a commitment to equity and excellence, and a culture of immediately applying new ideas. The coach, the principal, and colleagues are there to help. Teachers also engage the district expert to help apply practices. The system is a closed loop—individual, team, whole school, with team as the nexus. And in this particular case, the district is integral.

LEADING AND ORCHESTRATING PROFESSIONAL LEARNING TO SUPPORT PERSONALIZATION OVER TIME

Embarking on the Journey

Once a school has seriously committed to equity, they embark on a journey to personalize student learning. It takes several years to integrate personalized learning into classroom instructional routines and team dialogue protocols. Educators on this journey report that they are steadily improving how they integrate the work of teaching, learning, and assessment.

For example, when Montgomery Center School made a deep commitment to equity, they worked first on climate and then on establishing agreement on effective instruction. Working together in book study, they rethought how they approached setting learning goals, and then used their PLC time to develop assessments that were more tightly aligned to student learning goals. These mid-cycle assessments became the basis of a reteach block—formal time when students get additional help or extend learning.

From a professional learning perspective, reteach helped teachers think about what student learning looks like along the way, and to learn strategies to support each student and address learning needs of students regardless of their current level of understanding. As they developed skills to both teach and monitor student learning in the moment, they began to integrate reteach strategies within the context of regular instructional time. Over time, regular classroom instruction becomes a more personalized student learning experience. As educators have increased their skills in using data and applying it immediately, they now rely less on mid-cycle common assessments, and more on classroom formative assessment practices—real-time data collection and analysis that allows in-the-moment feedback on learning. The Montgomery timeline in Table 4.2 on page 88 illustrates how the layered work of deepening capacity to improve instruction develops.

Selecting and Supporting New Initiatives Based on Evidence of Student and School Needs

Neglecting capacity building because it is not mandated can set back or sabotage a school's trajectory. And blindly following the best-intentioned government requirements can be equally damaging. Each school community must discern the right mix of professional learning, and the right combination of theorists and frameworks. When needed, principals shield adults in the community from district messages that can distract or contradict a school's reform trajectory. This work includes and goes beyond that, as learning leaders proactively seek out new initiatives. As the right mix of professional learning needs is calibrated, leaders set about finding resources. Sometimes the district is a primary support; sometimes it gives school leaders reason for buffering. These are not mutually exclusive. Sometimes one or more external organizations are the primary professional learning partners external to the school.

Making Theories and Approaches
Relevant to Unique School Needs and Culture

All the schools focus on outcomes and best practice, yet they tap varying theorists, professional learning providers, and resources. Each featured school also started their journey using different strategies, and then iteratively extended their work over time. Content, pedagogy, assessment, and data use can all be the starting place for raising expectations or personalization. Focusing on one component with fidelity organically leads to the others.

Follow-Through and Persistence Until There Is Success

Leaders are careful to not overwhelm educators with too many reforms at once. They seek to provide enough time to understand, integrate, apply, and refine new practices or frameworks. They may advocate with the district to make haste in offering an innovation and related resources, or they may negotiate for additional time so they can implement fully and with fidelity. Leaders try to ensure new learning is introduced at a "teachable moment," when something is relevant and necessary to the next step in improvement. They also recognize that change happens at different paces for different people, and make room for that reality.

The substantial effort of helping educators contextualize and integrate new learning seeks to be responsive to thoughtful teacher questions, reduce resistance based on missing the relevance of the innovation, and demonstrate that an initiative was an essential next step. To do this, leaders are knowledgeable about new initiatives, and work hard to fully understand both their value as well as the likely challenges of implementation. At Montgomery, Mrs. O'Brien explains that "Common Core standards are coming," making the case for being ahead of the inevitable curve, while at the same time pressing the critical thinking and deeper learning that is necessary to their school's improvement.

The persistence and follow-through on big challenges is present in every school, whether it is a strategy for a specific child or teacher, or whether it is attending to a systemic low achievement. In the featured schools, when new approaches are introduced, they are practiced and refined until there is mastery. Teachers are supported through all the stages of their learning process. Leaders recognize that changing classroom routines takes significant time and that the primary goal—schoolwide implementation—must be met if equity goals are to be reached.

Figure 8.2 Leadership for Professional Learning That Advances Equity

Leadership for professional learning in some schools		Leadership for professional learning in schools focused on equity and personalization
Distributed leadership is generally encouraged.		Leaders formally share and divvy up responsibility for shaping and leading professional learning. They collaborate and use evidence of practice to establish the right mix of professional learning.
It is often not clear how new skills build on teachers' existing knowledge base.		Leaders manage the pace of implementation and scaffold supports to ensure new initiatives build on existing knowledge and skills. External requests are buffered or contextualized to align with existing goals and priorities.
Leaders have general knowledge of new initiatives. Depth of knowledge necessary to guide teachers to new learning may be relegated to outside experts, and therefore absent from day-to-day dialogue.		Leaders are knowledgeable about reform and seek out new initiatives. They guide and support colleagues in implementation, and know enough to bridge prior and new efforts for each teacher, team, and schoolwide.
There is respect for the capacity of educators to learn, and to innovate and experiment to improve practice.		Leaders ensure work is implemented fully, and that the right materials, resources, and time are in place so there are adequate opportunities to learn and practice new skills, until they are honed and integrated into daily instructional practice.
Hiring focuses on teacher as instructor; effective collaboration may be stated but without accountability.		Hiring decisions are based on candidate skills, knowledge, and dispositions, including the capacity to focus on data and personalize instruction, collaborate, and be flexible in service of students.

Maximizing Professional Learning to Support Sustained and Systemic Implementation

There are always priorities when making investments in professional learning. Here are examples of choices featured schools made:

Staff members attend external professional learning conferences/institutes when their focus aligns with school priorities. The people who attend have structured time to teach the full community what they learned. Everyone is then held accountable for implementing selected ideas and strategies.

One or two persons scout out professional learning resources based on understanding individual and group needs, then work on some fundamental concepts with everyone. When there's understanding of the effort at hand and readiness to go deeper, then the investment in an external expert can be made. To further maximize the use of funds, the expert can be contracted to work with the whole district.

Educators are liaisons to different educational partners, responsible for keeping the partners aware of school priorities, encouraging them to offer relevant supports to the school, and tracking on emerging opportunities and resources that may advance individual, team, and school priorities.

Professional learning leaders balance letting teachers learn what interests them most and ensuring school and systemwide goals are met, while providing structured expectations and mechanisms to learn one another's expertise and take responsibility for learning from one another.

Sustaining necessary resources. The formal administrators of the school are central to ensuring key resources: supports and structures to facilitate personalization. They include maximizing increasing professional learning time across the day and year (see box), identifying what supports are available and hunting for more, and organizing people and pupils to maximize learning. As one principal said, "That's my job."

Attending to educator effectiveness. Primary attention goes to ensuring educator effectiveness.[5] Having a critical mass of capable educators means having professional capital—the main resource that will assure student and school success. When a visitor to Montgomery asked if the educators there are more competent than those of other schools, principal Beth O'Brien reflected on the visitor's question:

I don't think that. . . . Maybe we work "smarter," but I don't think we are more intelligent. I don't think if we took our IQs against other people's IQs . . . I didn't know if "smarter" was the right word. . . . What he was seeing was that we don't just do things, we think about our practice here. And we reflect on our practice. . . . This is a purposeful decision . . . so that school improvement is like action research.

In the featured schools, teachers are supported by a system that encourages each of them to do their best possible work. "Excellent instruction" is less about having a full faculty of all award-winning teachers (Hargreaves & Fullan, 2012) and more about a group of competent teachers working together daily to practice, reflect, and improve.

Teacher hiring. Educators who come to these four schools generally embrace the mission and professional approach, and they tend to stay. Educators also know that it can be a challenge to find the right fit: people willing to try new things, to think deeply, and work together. Lead teachers from the high school reflect:

Mr. Austin	My original teacher job was in X [name withheld]. I was considered one of the best teachers in the school. I was not that good. I was really good in the group of teachers I was working with. I feel like I'm a really good teacher here,

but I'm one of many good teachers here.

Ms. Siegeler I only taught at one school before I came here, and I definitely had the feeling that I could get anything I wanted [there]. I want to teach this book, and the principal said, "We'll get it." I did feel a little spoiled because I was seen as a

---

Tending to Time

Learning leaders all recognize time as a central resource and used different strategies.

One school got permission to take the professional development time normally offered at the beginning and end of the school year and distribute the hours across the year to support ongoing learning and reflection.

The pilot high school has an elect-to-work agreement, has a longer school day, weekly faculty gathering time that lasts up to two hours, and a four-day, off-site retreat (paid for by a partner).

One school convenes teams twice weekly. There is a multigrade team meeting that attends to individual student needs, logistics, and teacher-generated issues. The second gathering is called PLC meetings, where teachers focus on data, and the instructional and assessment issues they generate.

Stipends are provided, when additional funds are available, for teams to complete curriculum work outside of school time. This allows for collaborative design of curriculum, instruction, and assessment, and ensures greater readiness for the short-cycle data review and intervention planning that takes place during PLCs.

Learning leaders support planning and follow-up of planning and other professional learning sessions to maximize use of regularly available time.

very good teacher there. Then, when you are in a microcosm [here] where everyone is exceptional, how much is exceptional, and how much is just the right thing to do?

The educators take great care to recruit and interview new staff members. Three schools start staff in part-time positions before hiring them full time when possible, grow them as student teachers first, or engage and cultivate people from nontraditional backgrounds. These methods create clear expectations and culture, and provide a chance to observe how the persons operate in the school.

One principal said, "I'm hiring for a personality." The schools seek a set of dispositions, but multiple educators say that listing them, even explaining them, does not necessarily get the message across. One teacher leader said, "Every school will say they are rigorous and everyone interviewed will say that they have high expectations. . . . Then you get to the class and there is coloring" (see Figure 8.3 for lessons on hiring).

While it's impossible to choose the perfect candidate every time, interviewees who are not a good fit tend to reveal themselves. As one principal put it, "We had varied beliefs along the way, and many chose another ZIP code to work in." Those who stay have solid skills and a value for the way learning for all is approached.

Systems of responsibility, accountability, and feedback, and prescriptions for professional learning. Leaders in these schools have established systems to tap intrinsic motivation, support it, track progress, and see efforts through to success. Intrinsic motivation does not mean that no one is checking to see if work is done. In fact, everyone tracks on progress *because* of intrinsic motivation. It keeps people honest and working to the same standards, together.

Collective responsibility for equity and excellence. School values, culture, and ambitious goals intersect fully when each person in the system sees themselves as personally responsible for equity. Each school has internal goals and systems that are often more ambitious than external expectations set by their district, state, or federal policies, or other external agents. Educators are not oblivious to external carrots or sticks, but they are also not governed by them. One teacher says, "It was never about AYP." A principal says, "The teachers are type A. If I'm not pushing, they are pushing. They are driving themselves."

Continuous learning. Educators in these schools understand that student success requires educators to become collectively responsible and

Figure 8.3 Lessons on Hiring

What to Look for When Hiring

- Evidence of collaboration and sharing responsibility for student learning
- Skill in using data to improve practice
- Eagerness to have colleagues in your classes, and for you to observe colleagues in the name of student and adult learning
- Flexibility: people with the right licenses and/or willing to get the right licenses
- Willingness to work hard

Interview Tips

- Show a video that demonstrates student and professional rigor in action
- Tell people they are going to work harder than they have worked before—and love it
- Include students in interviews and notice how the candidate responds to them
- Find out how much and what kind of collaboration and peer observation they have done, and explain with precision what yours looks like and requires
- Be clear that doing a good job in your classroom by yourself is not good enough

Interview Questions

- Are you here for the children?
- Are you coming to learn?
- You have to be a good teacher. What else can you do? What else can you bring to the table?
- Would you be willing to lead professional development?
- Would you be willing to be on the X committee? How could you contribute to that committee?
- Are you willing to have a colleague walk into your class at any moment? Are you willing to observe colleagues regularly to support your learning?
- What do you do if you see a student in the back of the class crying and not taking his test?

continuously improve their craft.[6] Systematic student success requires building professional capital across the school. In three of the four schools, educators personally offer colleagues support when they see someone needs help, whether they ask for it or not. Stults Road activates a system of support when a teacher fails to respond effectively to students who are not meeting goals on their benchmark assessment. The Instructional Leadership Team analyzes the situation, identifies ways to work with specific students, helps the teacher with knowledge or skills, and provides supplementary resources to extend learning. The teacher is involved. This process may involve a coach or administrator, but it may also start with a colleague, as it did in a first-grade classroom when the authors visited the school.[7]

Collective responsibility. Because the first, most important thing is students doing well, solid evidence that help is needed justifies asking for and offering help. Lead teacher Jeff Austin describes the markedly different approach: "I think the current paradigm [of teachers and teaching] is 'I have my little realm of teaching and that is what I do. And then my students leave and they go to a different room until the next day I see them.' Whereas here it just does not happen." The primacy of collective responsibility trumps the teacher tending exclusively to his or her own class. Systems ensure collective responsibility is employed. Mr. Austin continues in dialogue with colleague Samantha Siegeler:

Mr. Austin	You need to be able to make all those decisions with the student at the center of that decision, and not the teachers at the center of the decision, which is painful.
Ms. Siegeler	It hurts sometimes. It is exhausting sometimes, but it is the reason we work.
Mr. Austin	That's a difficult one. There's a balance, too. . . . At times, we do sometimes have to make decisions based on the teacher, but we're not going to be successful [as a school]. Teachers may say, "I want to teach this because it is interesting." But where is it going to fit in with the kid?

The power of professional capital. Schools that meet the needs of each learner require that every teacher participates continuously in professional learning, prepares thoroughly, and makes effective judgments using their knowledge, skills, capabilities, and experience. As these schools attest, leaders can change existing systems of professional learning to ensure that all teachers have the supports required to meet the needs of each student. And leaders can create opportunities for collaboration driven by educators, directed by student learning. Teacher teams in these schools are focused, work hard, and together make substantial improvement. Changing systems is demanding for school leaders and teachers—but as these schools show, when done well it drives intrinsic motivation and results in satisfaction with the craft,[8] which fuels additional learning throughout the system. Together these approaches raise the professionalism of the entire school, so that students encounter excellent teaching every day.

One principal summed it up this way:

It's not about great teachers or good teachers working in isolation. If we want to effect change, we have to have a systemic approach. It is not a competition to see if we can do better than the teacher above and below you; it is not a tug of war game.

Both students and teachers reap the benefits of increased professional capital. Many teachers enter the profession with a belief that they will be able to help all students. One teacher said that the personal value of being able to reach more students, and to do so with greater success, is "like crack." It is motivating, compelling, and it can also be addictive, egging on the teachers to learn more. Raising increased professional capital within the system results in increased satisfaction amongst teachers, which was evidenced across the school sites.

In all four schools, professional learning mirrors personalized, high-quality student learning. These schools have raised the rigor of professional learning, echoing our societal goals of rigorous student learning. Meeting the learning needs of every student is activated through leadership and learning systems that strengthen individual educators and school communities. The featured schools respond quickly to research-based mandates. But they do not just wait for the district or other outside authorities to come up with good ideas. The school communities build their own agendas, and leverage and customize opportunities in order to make equity possible.

Reflection: How does learning for students and educators work in your school? How are they similar to and different? What's a possible, next step for getting to professional learning that helps educators focus more on individual students?

To what degree are individual, team, and whole school learning intentionally aligned? What can be learned from the cases about professional learning in individual, team, and whole school contexts? How integrated and balanced are these three in your school right now?

How might your school deepen partnerships where principals and other lead learners model key values of collaboration, continuous learning, and collective responsibility? In what ways might this shared responsibility for adult learning impact student learning?

What is the role of leaders in your school regarding learning about and disseminating new instructional practices? What can extend opportunities for shared learning?

NOTES

1. See Hargreaves and Fullan (2012). Professional capital is the amalgam of human capital (an individual's talent and capacity), social capital (the talent and development of groups working together with a common focus), and decisional capital (the capacity to make complex decisions about practice).

2. Boykin and Noguera (2011) describe how the intent to focus on equity is not sufficient. While some schools attend to many characteristics of professional learning, very few schools are making strides in closing the achievement gap.

3. Dweck's (2006) research on growth mindsets describes that individuals who believe that intelligence is fixed will be more negatively impacted by failure than those who believe that intelligence is determined by working hard and learning to overcome setbacks.

4. See Dweck (2010). This idea is an underpinning of formative assessment practices, where subtle cues are provided about the value of understanding what the student does not know, and learning how to resolve learning issues as they arise through the use of evidence.

5. See Killion and Kennedy (2012) for a discussion of the connection between educator and student learning standards, and professional learning.

6. See Theoharis (2007). In his research on principals committed to social justice, Theoharis found that they have a "deep commitment to always looking to improve," and "a constant effort to re-examine our progress."

7. Costa and Kallick (1994) highlight reflection as central to understanding next steps. Self-directed learners demonstrate commitment to change by building critique and assessment into their everyday actions. By re-examining and clarifying various aspects of the values, purposes, goals, strategies, and outcomes, they continue to learn and develop an even more positive disposition toward continued learning (p. 7).

8. For a fuller discussion of individual teacher efficacy in the profession, and examples of professional practice that sustain teachers, see Nieto (2003).

Call to Action   9

While many teachers get a day or two of professional development on various topics, very few have the chance to study any aspect of teaching for more than two days . . . most . . . opportunities do not meet the threshold needed for strong effects on practice or student learning.

—Darling-Hammond, et al. (2009 p. 34)

ADVANCING EQUITY GOALS MEANS PERSONALIZING INSTRUCTION AND DEVELOPING PROFESSIONAL CAPACITY

The dynamics in the schools studied lie in sharp contrast to the national norm. Their focus and fortitude should not be taken for granted, especially given the riptide of shifting budgets and legislation that can take down the best of intentions and plans. These schools implement until capacity was really built, and then subsumed as the next level of work is taken up. They work to be engaging, exciting, caring, and challenging in the way each student understands those terms.

As a nation, we expect educators to attend to a set of highly refined practices to support. And we should. But since educating is nuanced when done well, like any craft, it requires ongoing attention and refinement. And because education of each child is a corporate endeavor, requiring the village of teachers and families and others, the attention and refinement needs to take place in company.

Personalized learning for students does not have to be the experience of the elite, reserved for independent schools and occasional teachers considered aberrations. Personalizing learning for students schoolwide can happen when adult collaboration and learning is central in the context of an ambitious equity agenda. It's about changing the way work in schools happens.

What Schools and Districts Can Do

1. Articulate a Definition of Learning for the Community

   A common understanding of how people learn, and how to go about learning, can ground a school or district, and it can be used to shape learning experiences for students and professionals. Adults modeling how they learn in the midst of students makes intuitive sense, and its implications can be powerful for everyone.

2. Cultivate the Commitment to Equity and Excellence

   Moving from having no values stated, to values stated but aspirational, to equity values that are enlivened by tangible practices requires intentional effort. Developing specific practices and rituals to understand who students are as persons and using evidence to understand them as learners can point a clear and precise path to every student getting what they deserve: a chance to be their personal best.

3. Commit to Ongoing, Professional Learning

   Teachers and leaders in schools are the most precious commodities in ensuring students achieve. Their collective capacity to learn, to collaborate on decisions affecting students and their learning, and to make schools increasingly more effective lies at the heart of improving student achievement across the country.

   (Continued)

THE NEXT WAVE OF FEDERAL AND STATE REFORMS: NO MAGIC WANDS

National and state policies can both help and hurt equity. For example, the last 2001 ESEA Reauthorization set out the equity goal of "No Child Left Behind" within the public education system. As a statement it was aspirational and inclusive. In fact, it only required that some students doing better in order for schools to have meet Annual Year Progress (AYP). Funding was problematic because of its paucity for the task at hand, and for more funds going to assessment systems rather than improvement of school practice. Some critics assert the policy discouraged more personalized attention to learning. "Many teachers scale back their efforts to differentiate lessons because poor student test scores may end up shaming the school, harming students' progress, and influencing teachers' evaluations and even compensation" (Cuban, 2012).

An important, new national goal for the educational system is on the table: Every student should graduate from high school ready for college or a career (U.S. Department of Education, 2010). There is still work to do in locking down the specific plan, funding, accountability, and deadlines. Right now, it is an ambitious and inclusive equity goal. Whether it is aspirational or actionable waits to be seen.

This next round of national and state reforms also features implementation of the Common Core and educator evaluation systems, which is likely to have a mixed bag of strategies that advance equity, and those that impede it. The Common Core does press for deeper learning of content; this will be a boon in many areas, though it does not cover all the content areas where students in the 21st century need to excel, and it should not divert educators from those additional subjects. Educator evaluator systems, if not used primarily to bludgeon teachers, can be lev-

(Continued)

4. Attend to Professional Learning at Individual, Team, and Schoolwide Levels

While this is happening at some level in many schools, intentionality about attending to the three levels, aligning them, and focusing them on equity can make a huge difference.

5. Ensure Leadership and Systems That Cultivate Professional Capacity

The steadfastness to student and adult learning can be challenging to sustain in schools where programs, funding, staff, and politics can be precarious. Regularized practices, when aligned and iterative, change the way work gets done so it is focused on outcomes, and on supporting attention to individual students.

eraged to frame out cycles of professional learning for individual teachers, and these can and should converge with team and whole school learning goals. There are efforts in play to articulate the progression of instructional effectiveness as teachers move from novice to experienced, in the same way that rigorous, personalized classrooms do the same for students. These initiatives too have yet to reveal themselves as goals that advance equity.

OUR RESPONSIBILITY

Like the classroom teachers who emphasize some strategies more than others depending on the student, we as professional learning leaders have the responsibility to implement required strategies and content. And we have the responsibility of discerning how these policies can be organized to serve our best hopes and plans for equity and achievement. Government policies and mandates, at every level, may help raise the bar of equity and personalization, but they do not set the ceiling on what achievement can be.

More Research to Do

This investigation is small in size, and there is more to learn about personalization and professional learning as key parts of an equity agenda. Some topics for further investigation include:

- Impact of personalization strategies focused on classroom instruction, and those that focus supports beyond instruction (extra help college readiness);
- Family involvement as a strategy for learning about individual students and how to support them;
- Impact of teacher collaboration in learning on students who witness this learning in an ongoing way;
- The focus, processes, and outcomes of short-term data cycles with different frequencies; and
- Comparative cost of professional learning that personalizes learning in different school settings.

That is left to us, as local communities, and communities of educators. We can discern the right mix of strategies, work on brave and doable goals, create supports that facilitate collaboration and shared learning, continue to use evidence, and do the next right thing. We must keep at it indefinitely, pausing to reflect, discern again, and celebrate the outcomes and the people along the way.

CONCLUSION

We conclude returning to the idea of the adjacent possible, where all new learning grows from what already exists, rather than manifesting out of the blue. This book speaks to how teacher after teacher, and professional learning leader after leader, live out this theory daily. They are attentive to patterns and reflective of evidence. They seek to pay attention to a range of ideas and then try the next right innovation that will help them move forward. As leaders of professional learning in our teams, our schools, our local communities and beyond, we are called to do that same thing. We are to notice how far we have come nationally in the path to equity. We are far from the days when college was only available to 10% of the population, all of them White men. And we are to notice what is happening now: As we push to increase the number of students who succeed, we hit a wall unless we take children, one by one, and put our heads together to make sure that they make enough progress toward high standards. And then we must recognize that for individual students to do well, individual teachers must and can do well, when they have professional lives that support tapping each other's genius and expertise.

The theory of the adjacent possible also asserts that there are some periods of time when a critical mass of people are thinking and talking about the same issues in different ways, and that these times are to be recognized and seized as unique moments when revelations and progress can occur. We believe that this is one of those moments. Many of the findings from these sample schools emerge in other studies.

We have framed the work of these four schools, and presented them alongside other important research, while offering the lens of professional learning, equity, and personalization. It is our highest hope that this lens provides a powerful way to understand and engage these issues uniquely, and advances the conversation, advocacy, and practice for helping each and every learner achieve their personal best.

Description of Online Resources

The companion website documents artifacts that were collected through the school site visit process. During the interview stage, schools shared documents, templates and tools as evidence of key practices. In addition, the website includes the authors' initial analysis of each school's state assessment data, documenting schoolwide results over time and analysis of subgroup performance.

Website documents can be searched by school name or theme. For resources provided by a particular school, users can click on the school name to access a full list of resources by site. The website also provides searching by the primary themes of the book: Equity, Personalized Professional Learning, and Leadership and Systems. The documents in these categories are outlined below.

EQUITY AND EXCELLENCE VALUES

Framing Documents That Describe Key Equity and Excellence Values

- Stults Road "How do you . . .," Excerpts from Stults Road Planning Documents
- Stults Road Supplementary Mentoring Program
- Social Justice Humanitas Pilot School Proposal
- Social Justice Humanitas Advisory Design
- Social Justice Humanitas Elect-to-Work Agreement

PERSONALIZED PROFESSIONAL LEARNING

Tools for Students to Document and Track Their Own Progress

- Stults Road Weekly Behavior and Work Habits Report
- Stults Road Student Profile

- Stults Road Picture This: Personalizing Learning to Grow Equity Shapes Professional Learning, Leadership and Systems
- Tusculum View Fifth grade Unit Organizer
- Tusculum View Third Grade student editing checklist
- Tusculum View Third Grade checklist for narrative essay

Tools for Teachers to Document, Track, and Communicate Student Progress

- Stults Road Weekly Behavior and Work Habits Report
- Stults Road Kindergarten Personal and Social Development Report
- Stults Road Targeted Instruction 3 week plan overview
- Stults Road Targeted Instruction Anecdotal Record Chart
- Social Justice Humanitas "Forty Assets Development Survey" results
- Social Justice Humanitas Individual Pupil Education Form (IPEP)
- Montgomery Math Summary Form
- Montgomery Reading Progress Form
- Montgomery Steps of Goal Intervention
- Tusculum View Student Data Review Form

Team Planning Tools, Communication Tools and Protocols

- Stults Road Targeted Instruction weekly planning template
- Montgomery Template for Identifying Potential Root Causes

Student Inventories

- Social Justice Humanitas Advisory Lesson Plan for Multiple Intelligences
- Tusculum View Fifth Grade Parent Reading Interview
- Tusculum View Fall Student Reading Interview
- Tusculum View Third Grade Student Strengths Assessment
- Tusculum View Fifth Grade Reading Interest Survey

LEADERSHIP AND SYSTEMS

Continuous Improvement Tools and Approaches

- Stults Continuous improvement reading vertical cadre
- Montgomery Middle School Student Survey Questions
- Montgomery Elementary Student Survey Questions

Evaluation and Walk-Through/Peer Observation Examples

- Social Justice Humanitas Observation form
- Social Justice Humanitas Peer Observation Action Plan
- Social Justice Humanitas Peer Observation Reflection
- Montgomery Summary of Goal Attainment Form
- Montgomery Professional Goal Growth Plan
- Montgomery Example of written feedback from Principal to Teacher
- Montgomery Walk-Through Observation Form

Developing Consistency Across Teams/Tools and Approaches

- Stults SMART goals for reading vertical cadre
- Montgomery Collaborative Consultation

Methodology

CONCEPTUAL FRAMEWORK

Each case examines the school's professional learning practices in light of our assumptions about research-based components of effective professional learning and equity, which were outlined in the *JSD* article, "Digging Deeper: Professional Learning Can go Beyond the Basics to Reach Underserved Students" (Gleason, 2010). The initial framework identified that schools making advances in equity attended to a range of practices and beliefs:

1. Effective, research-based "basics" of professional learning. These consist of relevant and rigorous content, appropriate learning processes, appropriate allocations of time to accomplish efforts, and supportive contexts for professional learning, including culture, leaders, systems, and policies.

2. In addition, schools "going deeper" would
   - Design professional learning that focuses on students who have been traditionally underserved and marginalized.
   - Use solid data to understand students as people and as learners.
   - Measure impact based on impact of the underserved, and keep at it.

Planning interviews and site visits were organized around this framework. After cases were completed, and the cross-case analysis was underway, this framework shifted in order to recognize emerging patterns and areas of emphasis. A new framework made way for schools' emphasis on values and practices related to equity, and for separating discussion of specific professional learning practices, and the leadership and systems required to sustain and evolve them over time. That resulted in the following framework:

Advancing Equity With Professional Learning

Equity and Supporting Values
Focus and drive daily practices

Personalized Learning for Educators
Facilitates individual student success

Leadership and Systems
Sustain and guide continuous improvement

Assumptions About Schools

This framework had a set of embedded assumptions about high-performing schools that came both from the research on effective schools and our own experience as professional developers working around the country. We assumed schools studied would have

- significant collaboration among teachers;
- experience with formative assessment, which we assumed was necessary to understanding individual student needs and strengths;
- a range of data they track on regularly, and over time; and
- demonstrated understanding of adult learning content and process for K–12 educators.

THE CHALLENGE

An important challenge that surfaced in evolving this framework, as well as the work overall, was calibrating how deep a description of student teaching and learning there needed to be alongside the information on professional learning practices. What we found along the way was that if we talked about professional learning practices without describing what was specifically happening or desired in classroom, the descriptions of professional learning were amorphous and vacant. Yet we did not want the book to be about interdisciplinary curriculum or formative assessment, but how to embed these and other practices that schools chose to personalize. This was an important struggle, and one requiring greater fluency if we hope to understand, and convince the public, about the specific professional learning that has to happen, and why.

SELECTION OF SCHOOLS

Criteria for School Selection

We set out to identify schools that had

- at least 40% of students eligible for free lunch;
- student achievement gains on state tests increasing over time overall, and narrowing achievement gaps in multiple demographic groups;
- other indicators of outperforming the district and/or the state;
- indication of the school personalizing learning for every student, rather than focusing more narrowly to particular underperforming demographic groups; and
- public schools that did not require a special admissions process. This eliminated magnets, exam schools, and charter schools.

As a group of four schools, we also set out to identify schools that

- represented both rural and urban schools;
- covered the K–12 spectrum;
- represented different geographic regions of the United States; and
- had a range of student demographics in terms of race and culture, and learning needs.

Identifying Prospective Schools

We scanned lists of school award recipients: Title I Distinguished Schools and National Association of Secondary School Principals Break-through Schools. Concurrently, we wrote to colleagues and organizations around the country sharing our criteria for schools. When receiving recommendations, we vetted them by conducting data searches on state websites, and looked specifically at school report cards, additional data sets, and state lists of high-performing schools, as well as school websites.

As prospective schools surfaced and were vetted against the criteria, we contacted principals to learn of their interest in participating in this work and to share our expectations and hopes for this project.

DATA COLLECTION

Data collection consisted of phone calls, e-mails, document review, web searches, and site visits that included individual and group interviews, classroom observations, walk-throughs, observations of team meetings and other professional learning experiences, and student interviews. All interviews used semistructured protocols and addressed the content, processes of professional learning, the leadership and support of professional learning, important external partners, and supports.

Before the Site Visit

Rigorous preparation was undertaken for site visits:

- Two initial conversations with the principal or multiple school leaders consisted of assuring that schools met the criteria, procuring a range of school documents that clarify and identify specific student and adult learning practices, and planning for a site visit.
- Extensive search and review of additional school information on the web, both general demographics, achievement data, suspensions, and other indicators on local and state websites, in addition to searches of school partnering organizations considered to be key by school leaders.

Site Visits

Table A.1 lists the specific activities conducted on the site visits, which took place between October 2011 and May 2012, and lasted one to one and one-half days. Field notes and recordings were used to capture all individual and small-group interviews and observations; field notes were used in observing larger group convenings. The Stults Road field trip only employed field notes. The nature of the site visits allowed for more interviewing at some sites and more observation of professional learning at others, due to availability of individuals and groups. Overall, we gathered sufficient data about the professional learning approaches and content, and about related leadership and systems from a range of sources. At least one classroom observation and a walk-through took place in each school. In total, 23 educators were interviewed, nine different teams were observed during meeting time, and seven teams were interviewed.

DATA ANALYSIS

Data analysis consisted of an extensive, continuous consensus process. Memoing was an extensively applied strategy in summarizing reflections after the site visits, summarizing findings at each site, identifying gaps in information, and organizing points for the individual case analysis.

Document review was also critical to corroborate information learned in interviews and on web searches. Key documents included school plans; professional learning tools, templates, and artifacts; policy and philosophical documents; professional learning opportunities the school engaged in; and information on partnership—as well as those that articulate student achievement priorities, plans for achieving them, and results that were sent before the site visit.

Case Development

The combination of reviewing documents, comparing memos on observations, and revisiting field notes and recordings led to one person taking the lead in drafting the case and analysis. The document went back and forth until consensus was reached, and the document was then sent to the school for member check. This was done by one to three persons at each school, depending on their leadership structure and who had guided the process to date. Again, memos were employed in explaining the review process, the request for accuracy of quotes as well, and the school's particular practices, values, systems, and leadership. School leaders reviewed the draft document and gave feedback in writing and in conversation; they reviewed for accuracy and clarity, as well as their own quotations. Their review and comments could also catalyze the identification of additional vignettes, artifacts, and details about key points. In addition, all educators from the schools reviewed and approved quotes.

Cross-Case Analysis

The cross-case analysis was the result of juxtaposing significant themes that arose in the findings of each case. This analysis led to reframing the conceptual framework, as noted above, and to returning to field notes and recordings, and sometimes school artifacts and leaders to fill in information gaps that appeared in reorganizing the data. Matrices (explained subsequently) were carefully developed, and assertions were backed up by school artifacts and quotes from educators wherever possible. Assertions were made based on these analyses, and quotes and data from fieldwork were also selected to underscore key points in the findings chapters. In addition, when key findings were backed up by examples of varied practices at schools, these were turned into boxed text in order to help readers imagine them concretely.

To better understand commonality across schools, we conducted analyses of the following:

- Driving values at each school. This was examined through straightforward use of matrices, and then juxtaposition of key philosophical and mission-related documents, as well as segments of interviews with leaders about equity and how it is played out on a daily basis.
- Professional learning practices that support attending to individual students as persons and leaners. While a set of common practices became quickly apparent during analysis, the way and depth in which they were employed was somewhat different from our experience in the field, and from what we understood as true from research. To understand these differences, we examined the balance of individual, team, and whole school experiences, as well as how these three existed in relationship to one another. We also considered how the process, content, and context of professional learning—a framework drawn from past work of Learning Forward—was different from more typical professional learning experiences.
- Leadership and systems. A return to interviews about sustainability of professional learning and student achievement improvement, and related matrices, led to these findings.

PEER REVIEW

Corwin organized a blind peer review that resulted in requests for additional vignettes on how the learning of individuals and groups of students was personalized through collaborative educator efforts. This led to engaging principals and other leaders again in November and December 2012, and asking them to offer such stories and check additional facts. They either offered them personally, helped flesh out stories from our original site visits and interviews, or reached out to colleagues to identify additional relevant examples of practice. These were added to the introductory chapters or those on findings, or exchanged with vignettes already present in the text.

Table A.1 Range of Data Collection During Site Visits

	Stults Road Elementary School	Social Justice Humanitas Academy	Montgomery Center School	Tusculum View Elementary School	Total Across Cases
Classrooms observed	Kindergarten classroom, walk-through	9th grade geography, 10th grade English, 11th grade science and English classrooms, walk-through	Second-grade guided reading, third grade, walk-through	Extended walk-through in an open classroom environment	6
Teams observed	Third- and fourth-grade team meetings (14)	Design Team meeting, vertical teams within whole faculty meeting (26)	Primary and middle school teams (7)	Data Team meeting (8)	9
Grade teams interviewed		Part of 11th grade team (2)	Middle school team (3)	First and third (6)	4
Other teams interviewed	Leadership team (4)	Principal and co-lead teachers interviewed (3)		Principal and academic coach with ESL resource (3)	3
Others considered key to professional learning interviewed	Principal, teacher new to the school, data specialist, assistant principal, parent coordinator (5)	Principal, two co-lead teachers, community partnership coordinator, special education teacher (5)	Principal, teacher newer to the school, two teachers veteran to the school (4)	Principal, teacher new to the school, technology coordinator, special education teacher, and counselor (5)	19

(Continued)

173

Table A.1 (Continued)

	Stults Road Elementary School	Social Justice Humanitas Academy	Montgomery Center School	Tusculum View Elementary School	Total Across Cases
Coaching session	K-2 teacher and coach			Fifth-grade teacher and academic coach	2
Students interviewed	1 student sharing work	24 peer mentors, 1 individual student	3 middle school students	–	
Total professional learning experiences observed	3	2	2	1	8
Total number of educators observed in professional learning experience	16	26	7	10	59
Total teams interviewed	1	3	1	4	9
Total adults interviewed	7	7	7	9	23

Bibliography

Argyris, C. (1990). *Overcoming organizational defenses: Facilitating organizational learning.* Boston, MA: Allyn & Bacon.

Argyris, C., & Schön, D. (1978). *Organizational learning: A theory of action perspective.* New York, NY: Addison Wesley.

Aschbacher, P. R. (1991). *What have we learned from writing assessment that can be applied to performance assessment in other areas?* Presentation to the ECS/CDE Assessment Conference, Breckenridge, CO.

Ball, D. L., & Cohen, D. K. (1999). Developing practice, developing practitioners: Toward a practice-based theory of professional education. In L. Darling-Hammond & G. Sykes (Eds.), *Teaching as the learning profession: Handbook of policy and practice* (pp. 3–22). San Francisco, CA: Jossey-Bass.

Bambino, D. (2002). Critical friends. *Educational Leadership, 59*(6), 25–27.

Banks, J. A. (2004). Multicultural education: Historical development, dimensions, and practices. In J. A. Banks & C. A. McGee Banks (Eds.), *Handbook of research on multicultural education* (2nd ed.; pp. 3–29). San Francisco, CA: Jossey-Bass.

Barth, R. S. (2001). *Learning by heart.* San Francisco, CA: Jossey-Bass.

Barth, R., Eason-Watkins, B., Fullan, M., & Lezotte, L. et al. (2005). *On common ground: The power of professional learning communities.* Bloomington, IN: Solution Tree.

Berg, J. H. (2003). *Improving the quality of teaching through national board certification: Theory and practice.* Norwood, MA: Christopher-Gordon Publishers.

Berger, R. (2003). *An ethic of excellence: Building a culture of craftsmanship with students.* Portsmouth, NH: Heinemann.

Bernhardt, V. L. (2004). *Data analysis for continuous school improvement.* Larchmont, NY: Eye on Education.

Blankstein, A. M. (2011). *The answer is in the room: How effective schools scale up student success.* Thousand Oaks, CA: Corwin.

Boykin, W., & Noguera, P. (2011). *Creating the opportunity to learn: Moving from research to practice to close the achievement gap.* Alexandria, VA: ASCD.

Bryk, A. S., & Schneider, B. L. (2002). *Trust in schools: A core resource for improvement.* New York, NY: Russell Sage Publications.

Conchas, G. Q. (2001). Structuring failure and success: Understanding the variability in Latino school engagement. *Harvard Educational Review, 71*(3), 475–505.

Conchas G. Q. & Noguera, P. (2004). Understanding the exceptions: How small schools support academic achievement of successful black boys. In N. E. Way & J. Y. Chu (Eds.), *Adolescent boys: Exploring diverse cultures of boyhood.* New York: New York University Press.

Conchas, G. Q., & Pérez, C. C. (2003). Surfing the "model minority" wave of success: How the school context shapes distinct experiences among Vietnamese youth. *New Directions for Youth Development, 2003*(100), 41–56.

Constantino, P. M., De Lorenzo, M. N., & Kobrinkis, E. J. (2002). *Developing a professional teaching portfolio: A guide for success.* Boston, MA: Allyn & Bacon.

Costa, A., & Kallick, B. (1994). *Assessment in the learning organization: Shifting the paradigm.* Alexandria, VA: ASCD.

Cross, T. L., Barzron, B. J., Dennis, K. W., & Isaacs, M. R. (1989). *Towards a culturally competent system of care: A monograph on effective services for minority children who are severely emotionally disturbed.* National Institute of Mental Health, Child and Adolscent Service System Program. Retrieved from http://www.mhsoac.ca.gov/meetings/docs/Meetings/2010/June/CLCC_Tab_4_Towards_Culturally_Competent_System.pdf

Cuban, L. (2012). Standards vs. customization: Finding the balance. *Educational Leadership, 69*(5), 10–15.

Dana, N. F., Silva, D. Y., & Snow-Gerono, J. S. (2002). Building a culture of inquiry in professional development schools. *Teacher Education and Practice, 15*(4), 71–89.

Danielson, C. (2006). *Teacher leadership that strengthens professional practice.* Alexandria, VA: ASCD.

Danielson, C., & McGreal, T. L. (2000). *Teacher evaluation to enhance professional practice.* Alexandria, VA: ASCD.

Darling-Hammond, L. (2010). *The flat world and education: How America's commitment to equity will determine our future.* New York, NY: Teachers College Press.

Darling-Hammond, L., & Bransford, J. (Eds.). (2005). *Preparing teachers for a changing world: What teachers should learn and be able to do.* San Francisco, CA: John Wiley & Sons.

Darling-Hammond, L., & McLaughlin, M. (1995). Policies that support professional development in an era of reform. *Phi Delta Kappan, 76*(8), 597–604.

Darling-Hammond, L., Ross, P., & Milliken, M. (2007). High school size, organization, and content: What matters for student success? *Brookings Papers on Education Policy, 163*(203), 2006–2007. Washington, DC: Brookings Institute.

Darling-Hammond, L., Wei, R. C., Andree, A., Richardson, N., & Orphanos, S. (2009). *Professional learning in the learning profession: A status report on teacher development in the United States and abroad.* Dallas, TX: Learning Forward.

Deal, T. E., & Peterson, K. D. (1990). *The principal's role in shaping school culture.* Washington, DC: Office of Educational Research and Improvement. Programs for the Improvement of Practice.

DuFour, R., Dufour, R., Eaker, R., & Karhanek, G. (2010). *Raising the bar and closing the gap: Whatever it takes.* Bloomington, IN: Solution Tree.

DuFour, R., Dufour, R., Eaker, R., & Many, T. (2006). *Learning by doing: A handbook for professional learning communities at work.* Bloomington, IN: Solution Tree.

DuFour, R., Eaker, R., & DuFour, R. (Eds.). (2005). *On common ground: The power of professional learning communities.* Bloomington, IN: Solution Tree.

Dungy, T., & Whitaker, N. (2010). *The mentor leader.* Wheaton, IL: Tynsdale House.

Dweck, C. (2006). *Mindsets: The new psychology of success.* New York, NY: Ballantine Books.

Dweck, C. S. (2010). Mind-sets and equitable education. *Principal Leadership, 10*(5), 26–29.

Elmore, R. F. (2000). *Building a new structure for school leadership.* Washington, DC: Albert Shanker Institute.

Fredricks, J. A., Blumenfeld, P. C., & Paris, A. H. (2004). School engagement: Potential of the concept, state of the evidence. *Review of Educational Research, 74(1)*, 59–109.

Gardner, H. (2000). *Frames of mind: The theory of multiple intelligences:* Philadelphia, PA: Penguin Books.

Gleason, S. C. (2010). Digging deeper: Professional learning can go beyond the basics to reach underserved students. *JSD, 31*(4), 46–50.

Glickman, C., Gordon, S., & Ross-Gordon, J. M. (2009). *Supervision and instructional leadership, a developmental approach* (8th ed.). Boston, MA: Pearson.

Hallinger, P., & Heck, R. H. (1996). Reassessing the principal's role in school effectiveness: A review of empirical research, 1980–1995. *Educational Administration Quarterly, 32*(1), 5–44.

Hargreaves, A., & Bruan, H. (2012). Leading for all: A research report of the development, design, implementation and impact of Ontario's "Essential for Some, Good for All" initiative. Council of Ontario Directors of Education, Ontario, Canada.

Hargreaves, A., & Fullan, M. (2012). *Professional capital: Transforming teaching in every school.* New York, NY: Teachers College Press.

Harvey, S., & Goudvis, A. (2000). *Strategies that work: Teaching comprehension to enhance understanding.* York, ME: Stenhouse Publishers.

Hattie, J. (2012). *Visible learning for teachers: Maximizing impact on learning.* New York, NY: Routledge.

Herman, R., Dawson, P., Dee, T., Greene, J., Maynard, R., Redding, S., & Darwin, M. (2008). *Turning around chronically low-performing schools: A practice guide.* Washington, DC: Institute of Education Sciences, U.S. Department of Education.

Hilliard, A. G. (1991). Do we have the will to educate all children? *Educational Leadership, 49*(1), 31–36.

Hirsh, S. (2009). A new definition. *Journal of Staff Development, 30*(4), 10–16.

Hirsh, S., & Killion, J. (2009). When educators learn, students learn. *Phi Delta Kappan, 90*(7), 464–469.

hooks, b. (1992). *Black looks: Race and representation.* Boston, MA: South End Press.

Hoy, W. K., & Tschannen-Moran, M. (2003). The conceptualization and measurement of faculty trust in schools. *Studies in Leading and Organizing Schools,* 181–207.

Jensen, E. (2009). *Teaching with poverty in mind: What being poor does to kids' brains and what schools can do about it.* Alexandria, VA: ASCD.

Johnson, S. (2010). *Where good ideas come from: The natural history of innovation.* New York, NY: Penguin.

Kannapel, P. J., Clements, S. K., Taylor, D., & Hibpshman, T. (2005). Inside the black box of high-performing high-poverty schools. *Report, Prichard Committee for Academic Excellence.*

Killion, J., & Roy, P. (2009). *Becoming a learning school.* Oxford, OH: National Staff Development Council.

Killion, J., & Kennedy, J. (2012). The sweet spot in professional learning: When student learning goals and educator performance standards align, everything is possible. *JSD, 33*(5), 10.

Kirst, M. (2011). California plunges into the unknown in expanding class sizes. *Thoughts on Public Education* blog. Silicon Valley Education Foundation, 4/811. Retrieved July 8, 2012, from http://toped.svefoundation.org/2011/04/08/california-plunges-into-the-unknown-in-expanding-class-sizes/

Klem, A. M., & Connell, J. P. (2004). Relationships matter: Linking teacher support to student engagement and achievement. *Journal of School Health, 74*(7), 262–273.

Kruse, S., Louis, K. S., & Bryk, A. (1994). Building professional community in schools. *Issues in Restructuring Schools, 6,* 3–6. Retrieved from http://www.wcer.wisc.edu/archive/cors/Issues_in_Restructuring_Schools/ISSUES_NO_6_SPRING_1994.pdf

Lambert, L. (2003). *Leadership capacity for lasting school improvement.* Alexandria, VA: ASCD.

Learning Forward. (2011). *Standards for professional learning.* Oxford, OH: Author.

Leithwood, K., & Jantzi, D. (2000). The effects of transformational leadership on organizational conditions and student engagement with school. *Journal of Educational Administration, 38*(2), 112–129.

Leithwood, K., Louis, K. S., Anderson, S., & Wahlstrom, K. (2004). How leadership influences student learning. *Center for Applied Research and Educational Improvement, University of Minnesota,* 289–342.

Lieberman, A., & Wood, D. (2002). *Inside the National Writing Project: Connecting network learning and classroom teaching.* New York, NY: Teachers College Press.

Losen, D., & Gillespie, J. (2012). Opportunities suspended: The disparate impact of disciplinary exclusion from school. *Civil Rights Project/Proyecto Derechos Civiles.* Retrieved from http://civilrightsproject.ucla.edu/resources/projects/center-for-civil-rights-remedies/school-to-prison-folder/federal-reports/upcoming-ccrr-research/losen-gillespie-opportunity-suspended-ccrr-2012.pdf

Love, N., Stiles, K. E., Mundry, S., & DiRanna, K. (2008). *The data coach's guide to improving learning for all students: Unleashing the power of collaborative inquiry.* Thousand Oaks, CA: Corwin.

Marzano, R. J. (2007). *The art and science of teaching: A comprehensive framework for effective instruction.* Alexandria, VA: ASCD.

Marzano, R. J. (2003). *What works in schools: Translating research into action.* Alexandria, VA: ASCD.

Marzano, R., Pickering, D., & Pollock, J. (2001). *Classroom instruction that works: Research-based strategies for increasing student achievement.* Alexandria, VA: ASCD.

McClure, L., Yonezawa, S., & Jones, M. (2010). Can school structures improve teacher student relationships? The relationship between advisory programs, personalization and students' academic achievement. *Education Policy Analysis Archives, 18*(17), 1–17.

McKenzie, K. B. et al. (2008). From the field: A proposal for educating leaders for social justice. *Educational Administration Quarterly, 44*(1), 111–138.

Miles, M. B., & Huberman, A. M. (1994). *Qualitative data analysis: An expanded sourcebook.* Thousand Oaks, CA: Sage.

Mindich, D., & Lieberman, A. (2012). Building a learning community: A tale of two schools. *Stanford Center for Opportunity Policy in Education.*

Mizell, H., Hord, S., Killion, J., & Hirsh, S. (2011). New standards put the spotlight on professional learning. *JSD, 32*(4), 10–12.

National Research Council. (2000). *How people learn: Brain, mind, experience and school.* Washington, DC: National Academies Press.

National Research Council. (2001). *Knowing what students know: The science and design of educational assessment.* Committee on the Foundations of Assessment. J. Pellegrino, N. Chudowsky & R. Glaser (Eds.), Board on Testing and Assessment, Center for Education, Division of Behavioral and Social Sciences and Education. Washington, DC: National Academies Press.

National School Reform Faculty (n.d.). Home page. Retrieved July 10, 2012, from http://www.nsrfharmony.org

Newmann, F. M. (1996). *Authentic instruction: Restructuring schools for intellectual quality.* San Francisco, CA: Jossey-Bass.

Newmann, F., & Wehlage, G. (1995). *Successful school restructuring: A report to the public and educators by the Center on Organization and Restructuring of Schools.* University of Wisconsin–Madison: Center on Organization and Restructuring Schools.

Nieto, S. (2003). *What keeps teachers going?.* New York, NY: Teachers College Press.

Nieto, S. (2010). *The light in their eyes: Creating multicultural communities.* New York, NY: Teachers College Press.

Nieto, S., & Bode, P. (2011). *Affirming diversity: The sociopolitical context of multicultural education* (6th ed.). Boston, MA: Pearson Education.

Noddings, N. (1992). *The challenge to care in schools: An alternative approach to education.* New York, NY: Teachers College Press.

Oakes, J., & Lipton, M. (2003). *Teaching to change the world* (2nd ed.). San Francisco, CA: McGraw-Hill.

Ontario Principals Council. (2009). *The principal as data-driven leader.* Thousand Oaks, CA: Corwin.

Payne, R. K. (2005). *A framework for understanding poverty* (4th ed.). Highlands, TX: RFT Publishing.

Picus, L., Odden, A., Glenn, W., Griffith, M., & Wolkoff, M. (2012). *An evaluation of Vermont's education finance system.* Prepared for the Vermont Joint Finance Office. Retrieved from http://www.lpicus.com/c5/files/2913/4543/4861/Picus_and_Assoc._VT_Finance_Study_1–18–2012.pdf

Raywid, M. A. (1996). *Taking stock: The movement to create mini-schools, schools-within-schools, and separate small schools.* Madison, WI: Center on Organization and Restructuring of Schools, and New York, NY: ERIC Clearinghouse on Urban Education.

Reeves, D. B. (2006). *The learning leader: How to focus school improvement for better results.* Alexandria, VA: ASCD.

Reeves, D. B. (2010). *Transforming professional development into student results.* Alexandria, VA: ASCD.

Robbins, P., & Ramos-Pell, A. (2010). *Shared leadership: A key to student achievement in an underperforming school.* Phoenix, AZ: University of Phoenix. Retrieved from http://cdn.assets-phoenix.net/content/dam/altcloud/doc/Teacher_Leadership_White_Paper.pdf

Robins, K. N., Terrell, R. D., & Lindsey, R. B. (2003). *Cultural proficiency: A manual for school leaders.* Thousand Oaks, CA: Corwin.

Rosenbaum, R., & Wrinn, K. (2010). *Starting points.* Retrieved from http://mydigitalsword.com/crea/education/

Saunders, W. M., Goldenberg, C. N., & Gallimore, R. (2009). Increasing achievement by focusing grade-level teams on improving classroom learning: A prospective, quasi-experimental study of Title I schools. *American Educational Research Journal, 46*(4), 1006–1033.

Scheurich, J. J., & Skrla, L. (2003). *Leadership for equity and excellence: Creating high-achievement classrooms, schools, and districts.* Thousand Oaks, CA: Corwin.

Schmoker, M. (2011). *Focus: Elevating the essentials to radically improve student learning.* Alexandria, VA: ASCD

Seashore Louis, K., Leithwood, K., Wahlstrom, K. L., & Anderson, S. (2010). *Learning from leadership: Investigating the links to improved student learning: Final report of research findings.* Minneapolis: University of Minnesota. Retrieved from http://www.wallacefoundation.org/knowledge-center/school-leadership/key-research/Documents/Investigating-the-Links-to-Improved-Student-Learning.pdf

Senge, P. (1990). *The fifth discipline: The art and practice of the learning organization.* New York, NY: Currency Doubleday.

Sharratt, L., & Fullan, M. (2009). *Realization: The change imperative for deepening district-wide reform.* Thousand Oaks, CA: Corwin.

Shields, C. M. (2003). *Good intentions are not enough: Transformative leadership for communities of difference.* Lanham, MD: R&L Education.

Sizer, T. R. (1984). *Horace's compromise: The dilemma of the American high school.* Boston, MA: Houghton Mifflin Harcourt.

Sizer, T. R. (1999). No two are quite alike. *Educational Leadership, 57*(1), 6–11.

Sleeter, C. E., & Grant, C. (2006). *Making choices for multicultural education: Five approaches to race, class, and gender* (5th ed.). Hoboken, NJ: Wiley.

Spillane, J. P., & Diamond, J. B. (Eds.). (2007). *Distributed leadership in practice:* New York, NY: Teachers College Press.

Steinberg, A., & Allen, L. (2002). *From large to small: Strategies for personalizing the high school.* Boston, MA: Jobs for the Future.

Talbert, J. E. (2009). Professional learning communities at the crossroads: How systems hinder or engender change. *Second International Handbook of Educational Change,* 555–571.

Tatum, B. D. (2003). *Why are all the Black kids sitting together in the cafeteria?* New York, NY: Basic Books.

Teacher Leadership Exploratory Consortium. (2010). Teacher Leader Model Standards. Retrieved from http://www.teacherleaderstandards.org/index.php

Tennessee Department of Education. (n.d.). Report card. Retrieved from http://edu.reportcard.state.tn.us/pls/apex/f?p=200:30:3324460927197276::NO:::

Theoharis, G. (2007). Social justice educational leaders and resistance: Toward a theory of social justice leadership. *Educational Administration Quarterly, 43,* 221–251.

Tomlinson, C. A. (1999). *The differentiated classroom: Responding to the needs of all learners.* Alexandria, VA: ASCD.

Tomlinson, C. A., & Allan, S. D. (2000). *Leadership for differentiating schools and classrooms* (Chapter 1). Alexandria, VA: ASCD.

Tomlinson, C. A., & Cooper, J. M. (2006). *An educator's guide to differentiating instruction.* Boston, MA: Houghton Mifflin.

Tough, P. (2009). *Whatever it takes: Geoffrey Canada's quest to change Harlem and America.* Boston, MA: Houghton Mifflin.

U.S. Department of Education. (2010). College- and career-ready standards and assessments. Retrieved from http://www2.ed.gov/policy/elsec/leg/blueprint/faq/college-career.pdf

U.S. Census Bureau. (2010). Profile of general population and housing characteristics: 2010/2010 demographic profile data—Montgomery town, Franklin County, Vermont. Retrieved from http://www.montgomeryvt.us/pdf/census genpopnhousing.pdf

VanTassel-Baska, J., Feng., A., Brown, E., Bracken, B., Stambaugh, T., French, H., . . . Bai, W. (2008). A study of differentiated instructional change over three years. *Gifted Child Quarterly, 52*(4), 297–312.

Vermont Agency of Education. (n.d.). School data & reports. Retrieved from http://education.vermont.gov/new/html/maindata.html

Vygotsky, L. S. (1978). *Mind in society: The development of higher psychological processes.* Cambridge, MA: Harvard University Press.

Wasley, P. A., Fine, M., Gladden, M., Holland, N. E., King, S. P., Mosak, E., & Powell, L. C. (2000). *Small schools: Great strides.* New York, NY: Bank Street College of Education.

Waters, T., Marzano, R. J., & McNulty, B. (2003). *Balanced leadership: What 30 years of research tells us about the effect of leadership on student achievement.* Denver, CO: Mid-Continent Research for Education and Learning. Retrieved from http://www.eric.ed.gov/ERICWebPortal/search/detailmini.jsp?_nfpb= true&_&ERICExtSearch_SearchValue_0=ED481972&ERICExtSearch_ SearchType_0=no&accno=ED481972

Wiggins, G. P., & McTighe, J. (2005). *Understanding by design.* Alexandria, VA: ASCD.

Yang, K. W. (2009). Discipline or punish? Some suggestions for school policy and teacher practice. *Language Arts, 87*(1), 49–61.

Yonezawa, S., McClure, L., & Jones, M. (2012). *Personalization in schools.* Boston, MA: Jobs for the Future. Retrieved from http://www.studentsatthecenter.org

Index

CORWIN
A SAGE Company

The Corwin logo—a raven striding across an open book—represents the union of courage and learning. Corwin is committed to improving education for all learners by publishing books and other professional development resources for those serving the field of PreK–12 education. By providing practical, hands-on materials, Corwin continues to carry out the promise of its motto: **"Helping Educators Do Their Work Better."**

Advancing professional learning for student success

Learning Forward (formerly National Staff Development Council) is an international association of learning educators committed to one purpose in K–12 education: Every educator engages in effective professional learning every day so every student achieves.

WestEd.org

WestEd, a research, development, and service agency, works with education and other communities to promote excellence, achieve equity, and improve learning for children, youth, and adults.